MICHIGAN
ON FIRE
2

MICHIGAN ON FIRE 2

by Betty Sodders

Thunder Bay Press

Thunder Bay Press

Holt, Michigan

DEDICATION

The effort that went into the writing of **Michigan On Fire 2** is dedicated to the forest fighting personnel of the Michigan DNR–Forestry Division and of the USDA–Forest Service.

Through their combined vigilance, Michigan has become a safer place to live.

ACKNOWLEDGMENT

**MICHIGAN DEPARTMENT OF NATURAL RESOURCES
PO BOX 30028 LANSING MI 48909-7528**

FOR IMMEDIATE RELEASE   CONTACT: Mike Paluda
10 July 97   906-228-6561

DNR FIREFIGHTERS RECEIVE NATIONAL AWARD

LANSING—In recognition of the strong support received from the Michigan Department of Natural Resources forest fire fighters during 1996, the USDA Forest Service presented an award to Michigan at the Natural Resources Commission meeting on June 5 for its cooperation in fighting forest fires.

The DNR, under an agreement with the USDA Forest Service since 1973, responded this year with over 100 firefighters to assist with wildfire suppression activities across the United States and Canada. Michigan firefighters were dispatched to 13 different states during the year, including Arizona, California, Colorado, Idaho, Minnesota, Montana, Nevada, New Mexico, Oregon, Texas, Utah, Washington, Wyoming and the Province of Ontario. DNR firefighters worked shoulder to shoulder with other local and federal firefighters to help battle numerous wildfires. Paluda emphasized that at no time was Michigan's ability to combat wildfires in this state compromised.

"This award, presented to DNR Director K.L.Cool at the June meeting of the Michigan Natural Resources Commission in Marquette, represents a tremendous achievement for us," said Mike Paluda, State Forest Fire Supervisor. "Not only did we assist other agencies in a time of emergency, but our DNR firefighters were able to test equipment, get valuable training and experience, and compare ideas and expertise with other wildfire agencies. The award is evidence that Michigan's impact in combating wildfire was felt and appreciated nationwide."

Presenting the award to the DNR on behalf of the USDA Forest Service was Randy Harrison, Fire Coordination Center Supervisor, from Radnor, Pennsylvania.

"Over the past few years, the DNR has been diligent about taking an active role in establishing agreements with local firefighters and other agencies in Michigan, so when a wildfire breaks out, not only is the DNR ready to respond, but numerous other entities can also provide invaluable assistance," Paluda noted. "This enables us to gain control much quicker, thus preventing wildfires from causing further damage to the resource or endangering human lives."

The DNR has taken an active role in the development of cooperative fire control organizations, including the Michigan Interagency Wildland Fire Protection Association (MIWFPA) and the Great Lakes Forest Fire Compact (GLFFC). The MIWFPA consists of the primary fire agencies in Michigan, and the GLFFC links Minnesota, Wisconsin, Michigan, and the Canadian provinces of Manitoba and Ontario in a cooperative fire control organization. Paluda noted that these organizations and agreements are essential in helping to address fire emergencies that may exceed any one agency's capabilities.

It has been only a few years since firefighters from across the nation came to Michigan to help with wildfire control duties.

###

Contents

List of Illustrations

Michigan On Fire 2

INTRODUCTION

The first volume of **Michigan on Fire** brought readers an accounting of Michigan's historic fires that reigned terror across this state between 1871 and 1911, destroying lives and property, leaving in their wake a path of total destruction.

In this sequel, **Michigan on Fire 2**, the state's fire story continues through the modern era. Starting in the early 1930's with the work of the Civilian Conservation Corps (CCC) and the building of fire towers, it traces fire's path of destruction at Fletcher Road, Mack Lake, Stephan Bridge, Stockyard, and more. The author's extensive research reveals the causes and consequences of the monumental fire at Seney in 1976 that charred 72,000 acres.

Along the way, readers will learn of the Roscommon DNR Fire Fighting Equipment Station...sit in on a test drive taken in a fire-equipped DNR Hummer...and take a close look at the problems between the National Guard's Camp Grayling and the surrounding civilian population over fire-related maneuvers.

Michigan on Fire 2 presents the costly and sometimes fatal errors made during fire suppression. This second book covers a wealth of territory and text and features success stories on and off the fire lines.

Bringing the Fire Story
Out of the Past...
Into the Present

*The first volume of **Michigan on Fire** brought together accountings of Michigan's historic forest fires; the Great Fires of 1871, Thumb Fires of 1881, coverage of Upper Peninsula fires including the burning of the village of Ontonagon, the Metz Fire of 1908, and the twin fires of AuSable/Oscoda. Companion material on efforts to fight these fires also was presented, from early Michigan Department of Conservation firefighting equipment to how homeowners today can protect their property from wildfire.*

*This first chapter in **Michigan On Fire 2** takes up the history of forst fire fighting where the first volume left off. It covers highlights of progress in the fighting of wildland fires, from the use of early fire towers to the able assistance of the Civilian Conservation Corps (CCC). Changes in the laws that help protect Michigan's environment are discussed in depth.*

Bringing the Fire Story Out of the Past...
Into the Present

Following the devastating forest fires prior to and around the turn of the century, fires continued to plague rural Michigan's northlands.

Notable fires following the AuSable/Oscoda Fire of 1911 included one in the vicinity of Silver City in Ontonagon County that ran rampant in 1923. Some 50,000 acres burned. In 1925, fires erupted in Gogebic, Ogemaw, Alger, Crawford, and Schoolcraft counties, claiming over 100,000 acres of land and forest. That same year, small fires dotted the Michigan landscape; combined, these burned over 600,000 additional acres.

photo courtesy Michigan DNR

Early firefighter (possible CCC worker) finishes ditching with a shovel...a firebreak was formed.

Chapter 1

Bringing the Fire Story Out of the Past...Into the Present

Although data is incomplete prior to 1930, the U.S. Forest Service has kept accurate records since then. According to a research document prepared by the Michigan Department of Conservation in 1950, during the period between 1930 and 1949, nearly 45,000 fires were reported that resulted in 1.3 million acres burned and $5 million in reported monetary losses.[1]

Early tractor ready for transportation to a fire

Early attempts to control forest fires involved action meant only to save property or lives. Methods employed in dousing a fire were the use of "bucket brigades." Sometimes water had to be transported with use of pack horses. Dozens of men using shovels were often the only way to attempt to slow down the path of a rampaging fire—the first line of defense.

Fire detection was nearly nonexistent unless a fire threatened a nearby settlement. Because of the constant fires occurring during the late 1800s as land was cleared for farming or homesteading, many fires were simply ignored because there was usually smoke on the horizon. Rural mail carriers often served as the first "fire scouts" reporting wilderness fires raging out of control.

Betty Sodders

A modern day Michigan DNR fire station. This particular unit serves DeTour/Drummond Island and is located at the eastern end of the Upper Peninsula. An early example of a fire tower appears to the left of the building.

Laws in the State of Michigan began to acknowledge the growing concern of lives and property lost to fires. Following the creation of the Forestry Commission in 1899, the first comprehensive forest fire laws were passed in 1903. These laws authorized the appointment of "fire wardens" as being part of a township's government. Wardens were afforded the responsibility of preventing and suppressing forest fires.

State control of Michigan's forests bounced between different commissions and offices for the better part of two decades until the Department of Conservation was established in 1921. Local control of fire wardens was eliminated at this time and the state assumed all fire control responsibilities and costs.

Detection of fires along with changes in firefighting equipment also went through many phases of growth and refinement during those earlier times. Lookout trees evolved into wooden, than metal fire towers. Eventually, fire towers were coordinated through the use of a communications system; first through phone lines; later by radio contact. Airplanes equipped with radios covered forest fire detection by the 1930s.

In 1928, twelve trucks were purchased by the state for use in hauling men and equipment to fires. Shortly following the development of the nation's first forest fire experiment station located near Roscommon, a new steel plow was created that would dig furrows to redirect fires.

Other law changes included:

1925: The burning permit law which also empowered the Conservation Department to prescribe regulations as to how and when burning could be done.

1927: A law authorizing fire break construction with 50% of costs paid by railroads, landowners, counties, and townships.

1935: Forest Fire Law of 1923 was amended allowing the Governor to proclaim a "no burning" situation when necessary.

1949: The laws were amended limiting the issuance of burning permits and making anyone responsible for starting a forest fire liable for suppression costs.

The legacy of Roosevelt's "tree army," the CCC, in Michigan was perhaps the major factor in bringing the fire story out of the past and into the present. Rising, phoenix-like, from the poverty of the Great Depression, President Franklin Delano Roosevelt's C.C.C., The Civilian Conservation Corps, fought for conservation throughout the entire United States.

The CCC began in 1933 and functioned until 1942, providing an important contribution toward forest fire protection in Michigan. Under this program, 70 federal and 56 state CCC camps were established; each held approximately 200 men. The Civilian Conservation Corps provided young, healthy, unemployed males with jobs. The men were paid $30 per month, $25 of which was sent home to their families. Most of their clothing, boots, and gloves were issued and room and board was included.

Both state and federal CCC camps were supervised by regular U.S. Army personnel. CCC camps consisted of a neat assortment of barracks, mess hall and outbuildings that provided accommodations for the work force.

While the Corps did not confine their activities wholly to forest fire control, this constituted one of their major activities. For

photo courtesy Michigan Historical Museum—Lansing

CCC workers fighting a wildfire

example; 95 lookout towers, eight cabins, 1,958 miles of telephone line, 24 airstrips, 6,818 miles of truck trails, 55 miles of foot trails, and 1,371 miles of firebreaks were constructed for fire control purposes. In addition, 207,410 man-days were spent fighting forest fires and 215,478 man-days were employed on fire prevention and pre-suppression activities. Inflammable debris was removed from 4,750 miles of road and from 167,265 acres of high-hazard land. More important, it was demonstrated beyond a doubt, that with adequate manpower and proper equipment, control of forest fires was feasible.[2]

Following devastating fires, CCC crews planted over 484 million trees. Today, the millions of trees they planted embrace our Michigan forested landscape. Harvests of second, third, and fourth cuttings are currently being realized.

The CCC's first and foremost priority was fire. During the 1930s wildfires proved common. With the formation of CCC camps throughout the north country, firefighting provided work for the 102,814 C-ers during their decade spent in the Wolverine State.

Fires were caused by lightning, sparks from steam engines' stacks, careless smokers, campers, and arsonists.

During the first CCC enrollment period, April–October 1933, Michigan state camps provided the bulk of their work aimed at fire problems. The second enrollment continued this endeavor. During that period fire towers were primarily built and over 6,000 acres of land cleared of fire hazards. Fire patrol…Fire prevention…became their watchwords.

Listed below are a few of the CCCs firefighting activities:

Unknown Date: Dana Lake Fire in the Hiawatha National Forest. No roads went into the fire area so water had to be hauled in on a railroad tank car by CCC-ers.

1935: A report estimated that there were 36,000 acres burned in the Ottawa National Forest. This territory was dotted with 38 fire towers.

1935: At Two Mile Creek near Watersmeet, (U.P.) all the CCCs in the entire area were called out—1,200 in number—to fight the fire with shovels, water cans, double-bit axes.

1935: Company 3624 from Camp Mormon Creek had three trained "fire" crews; the initial action crew, standby, and follow-up crew. Men were switched to different jobs weekly to ensure all would be proficient through the three phases of work.

photo courtesy Michigan DNR—Greg Lusk Collection

An early Michigan DNR wildland firefighter uses a pumper truck and hose to fight a small fire

1935: Camp Cooks, 686th company fought the St. Jacques blaze of 100 acres.

1935: Forest Lake fire in Munising district of the Hiawatha National Forest was handled by CCC firefighters.

1936: Hundreds of CCC workers spent the summer on Isle Royale fighting a series of fires that burned across 20 percent of the island.

1936: Cedar slashing burned southeast of Wetmore in the Upper Peninsula before it was suppressed, covering 3,200 acres. CCC men fought that blaze.

1936: Garden fire burned over 550 acres of timber in central Upper Peninsula.

1936: DuFour Creek fire burned over 900 acres. Walter Stokes, a CCC truck driver, saved ten men who were trapped in the blaze when he drove his truck down a railroad track, picked up the crew, and drove back through flames along the right-of-way.

1939: This year brought about one of the most terrible fire years of that era. The Presque Isle State Forest had 31,000 acres burn.[3]

As a memorial to the CCC units across Michigan, North Higgins Lake State Park located near Roscommon, has provided a Civilian Conservation Corps Museum. Memorabilia on display has been donated by CCC Alumni. An annual reunion is held at camp, during the second weekend in July.

The exhibits portray one of Michigan's proudest periods in its 150 years of statehood. The CCC played an important role in this history. Display cases and exhibits have been designed and installed by the History Division of the Department of State.

"This museum will ensure that the CCC's precious role in our state's history will be preserved and appreciated by future generations who enjoy the many natural resources, from forests to lakes, which the CCC gave us." said former Governor James J. Blanchard.

Today, as land values spiral ever upward, costs rise and budgets tighten. Wildland fire management combines cost-effective control with the use of fire in forests, brush, and grasslands.

In Michigan, DNR and U.S. Forest Service crews are short-handed and often are forced to use outdated equipment. The MDNR is spending $100,000 a year to upgrade vehicles, but should be spending $1 million a year. Prior to retirement, Greg Lusk, DNR's Assistant Regional Forest Manager for the Upper Peninsula, advised during an interview that the

photo courtesy Michigan DNR—Roscommon Fire Experimental Station
Modern-day forest firefighters mopping up after a blaze

Donald Haines

**A typical U.S. Forest Service weather station. At one
time perhaps a dozen such stations were positioned
throughout the northwoods.**

department's budget was so tight that many units were still using
20-year-old equipment...and parts for vehicles of such an age were virtually impossible to obtain. As an example he stated:

"The forest fire unit stationed at Crystal Falls had been using a
1966 Dodge W-500 4x4 that during 1992 had taken first place in
an antique auto show. Such action prompted the Lansing brass
to replace the aging truck, but due to super maintenance, that
truck was still in relatively great shape...even though it was next
to impossible to locate parts for it. Ironically, this vehicle was
later purchased by the U.S. Forest Service, which at the time
was having budgetary problems of its own, and they stationed
the aging fire vehicle at their Rapid River headquarters. At the

time cuts in both the DNR and U.S. Forest Service brought about a cooperation between the two departments…they had staff but no money for equipment…and we had the equipment."[4]

Today weather plays a major role in wildland firefighting. To better solve research problems such as prevention and suppression, scientists must understand how weather influences fire. Meteorologists today are searching for the most useful methods of measuring drought, a dominant force in past disastrous fires. They also study weather controlled phenomena such as fire whirlwinds and fires that spread quickly while crowning. By learning how to predict extreme fire behavior, they can improve firefighter safety and make suppression more elective.

As changes occur, former methods become obsolete. Bill Main from the U.S. Forest Service Experimental Station in East Lansing remarked, "Some years back, I traveled north once each year to personally talk with departmental weather observers. At that time we employed perhaps a dozen or so...that was probably about 1970. The person who took weather readings was deemed a person of importance, for they also served as cooperative weather observers for the U.S. Weather Bureau. Now times have changed...remote automated sensors measure the weather; satellites transmit pertinent data."[5]

Basically, today's forest fire specialists deal with fire research, fire weather, fire prevention, fire suppression, fire ecology, and fire economics.

Fire Towers

Where have all the towers gone? Today's travelers will find an easier task locating lighthouses than fire towers. Nearly all the former Michigan DNR forest fire towers have been dismantled. However, many fine examples still stand within the boundaries of the national forest system.

If you are fortunate enough to spot one of these fire watch towers, be sure to capture its image on film, for the few remaining towers represent the last of a former era...one in which towers served as a connecting link toward the fighting of wildfires.

Fire Towers

Forest fire prevention became a major concern by the turn of the century. Michigan's first steel fire tower was erected at Houghton Lake in 1913. A dedicated towerman was commissioned to sit atop the tower to scan the landscape for wisps of smoke. If fire was spotted, crews were notified. It was a solitary position.

Remember those steel sentinels of the forest? Not too many years past, fire towers were common landmarks throughout northern Michigan; today, few remain. One can still view a classic tower at the western limits of the Upper Peninsula, where the U.S. Forest Service's TeePee Tower stands at Kenton. Near Strongs, folks will notice the Raco and McNearney Lake Towers. At the far eastern tip of the peninsula, fire tower buffs can photograph the Goetzville Tower.

Jim Pudelko, retired MDNR Fire Officer, was one of the last towerman for the tower system and was assigned to duty at the Goetzville Tower. Later in this chapter, Pudelko will comment on his towerman activities.

At first, fire lookouts were little more than spiked trees with platforms mounted on top. One such tall pine stood near Raco until highway M-28 was widened in 1928. The lookout tree was later replaced with a steel tower.

The use of such vantage points led to the erection of small windmill-type towers with open platforms located along high points of fire patrol routes.

The first actual lookout tower in the state was a low wooden affair built by Northern Hardwood Manufacturers Association, that stood on a hill near Lewiston in 1912. The first steel tower was erected in the Houghton Lake State Forest in 1913. In 1915, a second tower was assembled on the Hanson Game Refuge located near Grayling. During 1916, three more towers were placed in the Upper Peninsula. Each year more towers were added until by 1924, over 100 fire towers were in use.

By 1925 towers with enclosed cabins appeared, replacing old open platform types; stairways were added instead of ladders, making towers more user-friendly. The tower system was virtually complete by 1928 and contained 107 cabin-type primary towers, 16 open platform secondary towers, and 19 open platform lookouts positioned in state forests or game refuges. By 1949, Michigan had 140 primary towers and five secondary towers in operation.

The standard modern tower was a specially designed 100-150 foot steel

Betty Sodders

Goetzville Tower, Eastern U.P.

photo courtesy Michigan DNR

Early tower operator uses an alidade for plotting a spotted fire, a pair of binoculars and a telephone. All were standard equipment.

tower with a glass enclosed eight foot square platform, from which the average effective vision range was 10 miles distant on a clear day.

Each lookout station was equipped with detailed surface maps; an alidade for accurate determination of direction from the tower to a discovered fire, and a telephone or radio, or both, by which fires could be reported to the nearest fire headquarters or conservation officer. A rule of thumb was to equate fire breakouts in relation to local landmarks. Distant fires were cross shots from adjoining towers. When visibility was poor, secondary towers were manned and during emergencies, aerial patrols were provided by either a state plane or by hired aircraft.

During the early years, qualification of a towerman was good eyesight and a knowledge of the immediate area. Lacking even a map, these first lookouts had to judge a fire by positioning with local landmarks and section corners. As tower numbers increased, fires were located by triangulation and accurate base maps were standard regulation.

Modern-day towermen also had to have good eyesight, be familiar with their territory, operate a radio, make meteorological observations, distinguish between unauthorized and legitimate burns, judge a fire's behavior, and serve as a good will ambassador to the general public. Communication became the tool of the modern towerman.

In 1933, the Department installed a number of two-way, medium-low frequency radio sets with a lab set up at Roscommon. Between 1938–40, over 120 battery operated radio sets were in place in fire towers, providing direct contact between towers and district headquarters.

Experiments with plane to ground radio communications began at Lansing in 1934 with the Michigan State Board of Aeronautics furnishing a plane and pilot.

Between 1933 and 1942, the Civilian Conservation Corps (CCC) constructed 95 lookout fire towers, eight lookout cabins, and 1,371 miles of firebreaks for fire control purposes. Their services also provided 1,958 miles of telephone line installation, that brought phone usage into remotely located fire towers.[6]

Historically, before the advent of fire towers and a communications system, it was easy to understand why fire wardens were able to accomplish so little in the way of forest fire suppression. Locating fires strictly by patrol proved akin to looking for a needle in a haystack. Certainly, Michigan's advanced fire tower system achieved the work for which it was intended.[7]

Prior to retirement, Jim Pudelko was assigned to the DeTour DNR field office, but when he hired on in 1965, he served as a Class-B Towerman. Pudelko relates his experience as a fire tower spotter:

From the time I was a young lad living a quarter mile from the Goetzville Tower, I longed to be a towerman…just sitting up in that 110 foot tall tower was strongly appealing.

I only worked about a year before being called into military service and upon my return, fire towers were being phased out, replaced by aerial patrols. I was transferred to the MDNR Forestry Division, under the title of Fire Officer.

As a towerman, we wore no specific uniform. We worked the tower only on high fire danger days, and even then, we did not man the tower until midday when morning dew had left the forest floor. However, if a fire was in progress, we stayed at our post from dawn 'til dusk.

Serving as one of the later day spotters, equipment consisted of a pair of binoculars, an alidade, radio and telephone. We also kept in an adjoining shed, 50 shovels and 50 axes along with a number of five gallon pump cans. All were marked with a CCC label. Each fall, towermen were responsible for removing large cumbersome radio sets from towers to prevent theft. This involved strapping a 20-25 pound radio unit to one's back and carrying it down the tower ladder. Some towers had stairs; Goetzville Tower had a ladder. It proved to be a difficult job.

We were issued a "tower key," which was a master key of sorts that fit any Michigan fire tower. If we were needed in any district, this key was readily available. I managed to keep one as a souvenir. Actually, our District alone held five towers including two located at Drummond Island. We performed maintenance chores such as painting stairways and making repairs to the cabin, and the keys provided easy entry.

When towers were replaced by spotter planes, they became obsolete. An aerial survey took in so much more territory, and a pilot could easily radio a ground crew advising them the easiest route into a blaze. If the fire was an arson fire, there usually was a two-track trail leading right up to its source.

Today, few towers remain across the state. The MDNR put them up for public sale during the 1980s. Goetzville Tower was purchased by the adjacent property owner. If I am speaking correctly, I believe towers sold for around $250 apiece. Many were purchased merely for scrap metal sales, not preservation.

We had an amusing incident regarding one of the purchased

photo courtesy Michigan DNR

Radio control technician handles tower talk from towerman to base station for fire reports

towers that was to be used as an observation tower by a couple from the western Upper Peninsula. They had bought a 110 foot fire tower and somehow a mistake was made and DNR personnel tore down the purchased tower. The couple demanded a replacement. When a tower was purchased, it was up to the buyer to have it dismantled and rebuilt; but in this instance, the Department had to locate a tower exactly like the one they paid for. A crew was sent out from Manistique and Naubinway comprised of Joe Anthony, Pat Clark, John Moon and myself to disassemble the Gould City Tower.

It proved to be a harrowing experience. The roof was raised

first. Everything had to be lowered to the ground by rope and pulley system. The four tower walls were dismantled which left us standing on the cabin floor 100 feet up in the air with absolutely nothing to hold onto whatsoever! Talk about being scared!

Flooring was removed next, then every step of stairway had to be taken apart and sent downward. Not even a wrench was dropped in error. But at one point, a cable slipped and instinctively I made a grab for it, but at the final second I pulled back. Had I not, I would have been pulled right down to the ground. As it was, the attached rod fell with such speed it buried itself in the ground just narrowly missing the man standing below handling the ropes.

Crosspieces were the last to come down, then the supports…it proved to be an immense undertaking.

So today when you have an opportunity to view one of these old fire towers, stop and remember how important they once were to the State of Michigan. In essence, they were our first line of defense against the constant threat of forest fire. I am proud that I had the opportunity to be a part of history in the making."[8]

While Jim Pudelko was one of the last towermen hired, research indicated that the ranks of towermen included one woman. The following story comes from an old newspaper clipping dated December 14, 1925 from an unknown source.

Girl Fire Sentinel Keeps Tower Vigil in Heart of Michigan Forest Wilderness

Harrietta, Mich. Dec. 14—Miss Lyla Ogden, Michigan's only fire towerwoman, who spends her hours from dawn to dusk 65 feet above ground overlooking a forest wilderness, won her appointment as a regular employee of the conservation department because of her fine record when guarding the tower during the long illness of her father, the late Charles Ogden of Harrietta, Wexford Co.

Miss Ogden, a university girl and a truly feminine young woman of 23, bobs her hair, uses a powder puff, and wears khaki knickers, when on duty, which is daily during the season from April 15 to the fall closing, usually October 15. This year, it was extended, owing to the drought and the raging forest fires in the north. Rainy days are holidays, however.

Office on Tower's Top

Her office is the top of the tower, 65 feet in the air, a room seven feet square, enclosed four feet up for the floor, with 32 glass windows above the enclosure. She climbs it on the ladder that runs up the side, dinner pail in one hand, and hoists her flag when she reaches the top. The flag is the signal of the

Betty Sodders

Raco Tower, one of the first U.S. Forest Service towers erected. An unusually small steel tower that sets upon a small hill, it can be viewed from Highway M-28 west of Raco's Ranger Road.

towerman's presence in the tower, and is furled when the towerman descends. Off in the distance a field man is watching, and he calls on the phone frequently.

None of the little things that a woman loves to have about her for idle moments may be taken into the tower by the towerwoman. Her duty is to watch the forests all about her, and to locate and report the moment she sees streamers of smoke in the woods. She may not read, or write, or tat.

Anything that tends to hold her interest and keep her eyes from the miles of wilderness about her, is discouraged by the rules that govern the office. It is a man's job, and Miss Ogden does it like a man. It pays $3.50 a day for the spring and summer months.

There is a feminine touch, however, in the room from which peer the eyes of the region. Miss Ogden has a rocking chair. There are other chairs there also, as state officials come there in the course of their duties, and no towerman is required to stand all the hours of the day.

Lives in Village

Every dangerous point in the district of which Miss Ogden's tower is a part, is covered by fire towers. It is one of a chain starting 18 miles east of Manistee, the district being one of 20 in the state. Miss Ogden lives with her mother in the village of Harrietta, a mile away from the tower, and drives to and from work.

She makes daily reports to the district warden, Mark Craw, of Traverse City. From April 13 to September 1, there were 302 fires reported in the district which is comprised of eight counties. Many were reported by Miss Ogden, whose accuracy has been favorably commented upon by the conservation officials.

Her work is not just a job. She has enthusiasm for it, and serves it with undivided attention. Neither fear, boredom, nor loneliness have come to her in her room on top of the tower.[9]

Bog Fires Had a History of Seemingly Burning Forever

In the history of forest fire fighting, bog fires have always presented special problems. They must be handled in specific manner or they appear to burn forever.

In this chapter, retired fire officer Lyman Beech of Tawas City shares his experiences fighting these most unusual wildfires. He describes his inventiveness in creating a revolutionary method for putting out stubborn bog blazes.

Bog Fires Had a History of
Seemingly Burning Forever

The fire burned so deeply into the peat bogs near Cedar River that it was still smoldering a year later. At times, during that first winter, smoke came up through the snow. *Michigan On Fire–Book 1*[10]

The above description of the Cedar River bog fire occurred during The Great Fires of 1871, which struck parts of Menominee County. That type of situation held true well into modern times, for there were no adequate means available to combat such stick-in-the-muck blazes until the 1940s.[4]

Retired Fire Officer Lyman Beech of Tawas City has had a great deal of experience in fighting bog fires. Former Governor William Milliken presented Beech with an award plaque and a check for $1,000 for his work in developing a unique control measure designed to suppress stubborn bog, muck or marsh fires. His procedure became a "first" in Michigan firefighting control history.

Fire Officer Beech shared much of his knowledge:

Bogs display a gradual development of a wetlands area slowly transgressing from open water to forested land. As mosses and sedges tend to encircle pools of water, shrubby growth appears, supported by floating masses of vegetation that actually penetrate farther toward the center. As eons pass, a bog undergoing these habitat changes, tends to dry out....mosses become peat...spruces and tamaracks invade the area.

Bog fires vastly differ in scope from conventional wildfires. If water is employed, the blaze will successfully be knocked down, but as ash is deposited, fire will continue to smolder deeply down under the ground, which results in constant flare-ups.

Chapter 3
Bog Fires Had a History of Seemingly Burning Forever

Early mulch fires generally were started by blueberry pickers that invaded such areas in search of berries. At one time, wild Michigan berries were sold commercially and special trains dropped pickers off along rail lines adjacent to blueberry bogs and marshes. At the end of the day, they boarded the train on its return trip. During breaks, pickers often smoked cigarettes, cigars or pipes. Ash deposited on the ground lay smoldering until a breeze might have tweaked it into flame. Afterwards, available flammable material caught fire.

If a bog fire is covered with mineral soil, it will remain hot. But, if you turn Mother Nature around and allow her to work against herself, a bog or muck fire becomes easier to extinguish.

Lyman Beech explained that prior to the perfection of his "natural"

Fire Officer Lyman Beech

A bog fire slowly smoldering

method, it was deemed to be a departmental taboo to add fuel to forest fires regardless of any given circumstance.

Beech developed a procedure by which a bulldozer was used to plow an entire perimeter of a peat bog fire. Both peat and mulch served as insulation. No water was required. The heat created at the bottom of the ash caused steam and as moisture traveled upwards through peat and mulch, steam cooled, turning to water or at least became heavy moisture. In turn, the fire literally put itself out.

Fire Officer Lyman Beech

Two bulldozers working a smoldering bog blaze; they are attempting to turn over peat/mulch by placing the mixture atop the fire, allowing it to put itself out.

The steam rose, then cooled within a two hour period following an application of peat/mulch during a bog blaze. Since heat evaporates water, the peat cooled, and the next day any remaining "hot spots" were easily visible and could be treated accordingly.

Before this method of fighting bog fires was implemented, a bog fire fought with water cost the Michigan Department of Natural Resources about $845 per acre. When Fire Officer Beech's bog fire technique was refined during the 1940s, departmental costs dropped dramatically to approximately $165 per acre. This development earned Lyman Beech the Governor's Award as previously mentioned.

Former Fire Officer Beech stated that he had been stationed in Michigan's Thumb area during most of his career. Headquartered at Port Huron, he estimated that during time spent in the Michigan DNR, he probably worked at least twenty bog fires. One extremely stubborn conflagration occurred prior to Memorial Day and lasted thirty days. It smoldered in a marsh near Sandusky. The year was 1970 and the fire took in some seventy acres of bog.

Beech also advised that numerous bog or marsh flare-ups can be contributed to lightning strikes. For example: A bolt of lightning might strike a barbed-wire fence, then travel along the wires charring or burning each and every fencepost during its fiery high wire act. Should field debris, tall grasses, or weeds be growing adjacent to the fence line, fire may ignite this material and quickly sweep a field, yet actually not burn anything in its path unless the fire collides with a pocket nest of a gopher, mouse or even a yellow jackets' ground nest. If this event takes place, the fire will continue to travel beneath the surface of the earth where it will continue to smolder. A similar scenario can be played out in a marsh or bog habitat.

While fighting a muck fire that erupted near the Thumb village of Deckerville, Fire Officer Beech was severely burned. He explained,

"Muskrats had constructed deep burrows in the banks along a ditch where firefighters were pumping water. A large pool of water had formed directly over part of the bog and suddenly, as though a plug was pulled, the water went down. In turn, hot coals and steam was blown upwards through a bank rat's "breather" hole and erupted full force directly in my face. At the time I was operating the bulldozer and instinctively, I put my hands over my face to shield it from the flames, while at the selfsame moment I breathed in deeply...scorching my lungs."

Shortly following the unfortunate incident, Lyman Beech accepted retirement.

An interesting sidenote occurred while a marsh fire was being suppressed in the St. Clair Flats located near Harsen's Island. A giant Canada goose remained on her nest setting her clutch of eggs as wildfire crews

Fire Officer Lyman Beech

View of a bog fire showing steam rising

bulldozed fire lanes along each side of her nesting area. Later, workers discovered the goose had successfully hatched eight tiny goslings shortly after the fire had passed.

Every fire story appears to hold a human interest happening. Lyman Beech enjoyed sharing that natural recollection as he concluded his discussion on bog and marsh fires.

The Fletcher Road Fire

On May 8, the Fletcher Road fire in Kalkaska County consumed 4,692 acres. The Fletcher Road fire was caused by a pipeline welding crew of the Curran Construction Company, which paid a total of $91,216.84 in timber damages and suppression costs. This was the largest claim ever to be collected for a forest fire in Michigan's history.

1968 Annual DNR Fire Report

Recalling the Fletcher Road Fire...

During a recent visit, Lyman Beech, retired Michigan DNR fire officer, recalled the sights and sounds of the Fletcher Road fire that records indicate burned a total of 4,700 forested acres in 1968.

Beech advised that even during its earliest stages, the Fletcher Road fire remained absolutely spectacular. Smoke could be seen for twenty miles as folks nervously watched the enormous dense black cloud rising.

Fire Officer Lyman Beech

Fletcher Road fire as viewed from a distance of three miles

Fire officer Beech brought slides and projector to the interview and as they moved along the track, he explained each one thoroughly. Many of the pictures were shot from a distance of three miles, though they appeared to be much closer. In numerous scenes, fire was depicted as it jumped across roadways, which under normal circumstances tend to serve as suitable fire breaks. One typical slide detailed the perimeter of the fire and showed flames approaching Fletcher Road itself. Today there are 1.9 miles of burned ground still evident along the sides of this road—scars left behind from that fast, roaring blaze.

Fire Officer Beech commented, "The Fletcher Road Fire began May 8, 1968 at approximately 2:45 P.M. and burned 4,216 acres across Kalkaska and Crawford counties with almost total tree mortality. The fire crowned in over seventy-five percent of the burned area."

Once the fire crossed Fletcher Road, it continued to burn at an estimated rate of some two miles per hour. The total length of the

Fire Officer Lyman Beech

DNR fire-equipped plane, the Beaver, prepares for a water drop as smoke billows forth from the Fletcher Road fire

ravaged area was perhaps six miles in length, most of which burned during a period of just six hours. It was regarded as being a fast fire—crown fires usually are. One later year report claimed, "Crown fires—those fires burning up into the tops of dry pines...can cover ground at great speed especially during high winds."[11]

The Michigan DNR fire-equipped airplane, fondly nicknamed "The Beaver," was pressed into action. The plane made a total of fifty-three water drops during the course of this fire. However, still another fire was reported that same day, and in turn, the Beaver serviced that blaze as well—in a sense, pulling double-duty. The second fire burned 1,659 acres and its cause was fabled as being the work of an arsonist.

During the slide presentation, Lyman Beech described a fire scene that depicted crowning action and displayed the intensity of heat traveling along the ground. He advised that this particular picture afforded credence to the concept proposed by Canadian Charles Van Wagner, that crown fires need the heat assistance of burning fuels located at ground levels to allow fire to be propagated into crowns.[12] Some slides showed crowning action leaping 100–125 feet high; others were taken with fire action depicting a slight delay in crowning as fire followed a running-ground mode.

Fire Officer Lyman Beech

DNR personnel and fire truck on the fire line—note Fletcher Road is blocked off from traffic

One slide bears the appearance of having been taken at night; but Beech remarked that the picture was shot during mid-afternoon when extremely heavy dense smoke blackened out all signs of daylight.

An interesting aspect of crown fires is that complete tree defoliation usually occurs during the action of such a volatile conflagration. Such a fire burns extremely hot, literally lapping up every speck of dryness along its path of destruction. Much of the 4,000 plus acres involved appeared to be completely defoliated after the blaze was extinguished.

Lyman Beech recalled two values protected during the Fletcher Road fire. One was a gas-cracking plant threatened as the fire came within a half mile of their holdings. This facility was estimated to have a worth of $1 million.

The second value salvaged during the fire's rampage proved to be a very special forty acre plot of forest land, planted in honor of one of Michigan's past governors, David H. Jerome, who served the state from 1881 to 1883. The forty acre parcel was planted in 1931 under a reforestation plan sponsored by *The Detroit News*. Several similar plots were completely burned during the fire.

The fire's aftermath brought about a thorough investigation. Fires, like weather phenomena, are far better understood after the fact. In this particular instance, a break in the continuity of fuels was illustrated, showing fringe areas along fire breaks that simply did not ignite. It was believed that the lack of supporting ground fires in some specific areas prevented crowns from lighting. There was no absolute proof to support this conclusion, but Lyman Beech strongly felt that once again the theory of Charles Van Wagner could be put into play here. Further investigative work was scheduled.

Aerial photographs showed views of the Fletcher Road fire where distinct fingers and islands of forest land were virtually untouched by flames. Another aerial shot pointed out the magnitude of the fire as it surveyed the major axis of the blaze. Once again, wavelike action could not be explained. It presents interesting possibilities toward future research, for no one has yet satisfactorily explained why this particular pattern of intense burning left behind unburned fuel throughout island clumps and finger spits of wooded terrain.

Other photos clearly illustrate the fact that both sides of a sand trail road were obviously scorched but not burned, for pine needles lay untouched in the fire's wake. Once again, this fact points out the theory that to crown, a fire requires ground fuel for support.

An additional form of post-fire phenomena was presented when columns of black dust were carried aloft to altitudes of 400–500 feet above ground level. Thousands of tornadolike wisps of debris were generated during the days that followed the fire.[13]

Excerpt From: Horizontal Roll Vertices and Crown Fires

By Donald A. Haines, North Central Forest Experiment Station, Forest Service, U.S. Department of Agriculture, East Lansing,, MI, February 5, 1982

Abstract:
Observational evidence from nine crown fires suggests that horizontal roll vortices are a major mechanism in crown-fire spread. Post-burn aerial photography indicates that unburned tree-crown streets are common with crown fire. Investigation of the understory of these crown streets after two fires showed uncharted tree trunks along a center line. This evidence supports a hypothesis of vortex action causing strong downward motion of air along the streets.

Fire Officer Lyman Beech

The fire approached Fletcher Road proper

1. Introduction

A wildland crown fire is usually short-lived but extremely dangerous and potentially catastrophic. Because most people near crown fires are either totally occupied with fire suppression or with survival, there are few reliable observations of this phenomenon. Van Wagner (1977) found little published on the behavior of crown fires except for reports of rates-of-spread and aspects of fuel arrangements. Without adequate observations, it is difficult to expand on the physical theory of crown-fire spread. Without a more inclusive theory, modeling is difficult and, consequently, reliable fire-behavior prediction is impossible.

2: Crown Fires

In the classical view, crown fire advances from top to top of trees or shrubs and appears to be more or less independent of surface fire. In a more elaborate model, Van Wagner (1977) suggested that crown fire depends on three simple crown properties: height above ground foliar bulk density, and foliar moisture content. He proposed classifying crown fires as passive, active, or independent according to their degree of dependence upon surface fire. In the passive classification, the crown phase depends completely on the surface fire, whose spread rate controls the whole fire. If active, the surface and crown fires must travel together as a unit. If independent, the crown fire can supply the required heat flux by itself and no longer depends upon the surface fire.

Crowning is most often a phenomenon of conifer forests...On typical freeburning fires the spread is uneven, with the main spread moving with the wind. This forward fire perimeter is the most rapidly moving portion and is designated the head of the fire. The adjoining portions of the perimeter at right angles to the head are called the flanks, and the slowest portion (that may be backing into the wind) is called the rear.

3. Case Histories
Author's Note: This chapter will only include the case history for the Fletcher Road fire. The other Michigan case history is Mack Lake Fire and can be found in Chapter 8.
b. The Fletcher Road Fire
Air photographs of this Michigan jack-pine fire reveal patterns of treecrown streets similar to those seen at Mack Lake. But one photograph of the Fletcher Road fire shows curved tree-crown streets in concentric bands near the point of fire origin, a feature not nearly as prominent at Mack Lake.

Twelve years after the Fletcher Road fire, a 1980 ground survey through crown streets where the conifer trees survived revealed faint but still identifiable tree scorch. The pattern was the same as at Mack Lake. We identified streets by walking between trees with char on the backside of the trunks and low branches but no char on the inside, at least above 0.3 m.

We could not locate the curved bands of crown streets. Apparently most crowns in this area were so badly scorched that few trees survived the fire. We were able to identify one curved, uncharred street, but it ended in an area of dead and down trees after a short distance.[14]

Author's Note: A table providing information on crown fires that indicated action of horizontal roll vertices listed the following information on the Fletcher Road Fire:

Fletcher Rd	Kalkaska County Michigan	8 May 1968	1900 acres burned	Primary fuels: Sapling to small pole jack pine	Temp=21°C RH=24–30% Wind=24kmh

Prescription for Fire

What is a prescription for fire? This detailed chapter describes the need for controlled burns. Today's fire prescriptions are meticulously applied; if all parts do not equal the whole, the prescription for fire is withdrawn.

In a sense, we have learned from past errors, and examples of these mistakes are also presented in this chapter.

Prescription for Fire

Terminology: Prescribed fire…fire monitor…ignition specialist…fire support module…fire line…torch fuel-mix cans… bladder bags…cubies of water…drip torch… strip of fire…nurse tanker…spot fires

Ben Jacobs, National Park Service's prescribed fire module program coordinator stated in a recent issue of *Wildland Firefighter* magazine, "The more we understand how fire is part of the ecosystem, the more we realized we needed to stop excluding it and start taking actions to reintroduce it."[15]

At the U.S. Forest Service work station located in the eastern Upper Peninsula, north of Raco, Forestry Technician Tom Kurtz, explained reasons and methods behind prescribed burns. The photographs shown in this chapter were also provided by Kurtz.

One of their prescribed burns was undertaken to reduce prolific growth of Reindeer Moss. A lichen growing 2–4 inches in height, Reindeer Moss appears in large round gray clumps producing stems that appear to branch out like antlers containing wooly surfaces and fingerlike tips. This lichen chooses to grow in northern sandy soil, dominating sand plains. In this habitat, a prescribed burn encourages blueberry growth and grassland development. Reindeer Moss burns readily.

Prescribed burns are often used to remove unwanted jack pine. During such a fire, young aspen trees tend to quickly regenerate after burning, which vastly improves deer habitat.

When understory burning for natural regeneration of red pine, pines are first selectively thinned before the burn takes place. The prescribed burn prepares the seed bed causing cones to react to the heat. They burst and then scatter.

Tom Kurtz advised, "Timing is critical for controlled burns to produce desired results. Prescribed burns prove easier when conducted with some snow cover still on the ground...they employ a smaller holding force...provide a less expensive, safer method of burn. But all prescribed burns hold a specific purpose; some are more efficient when conducted during summer or fall months. The method must fit the need."

Fire Specialist Kurtz continued, "First, a backing fire is laid down to serve as buffer. Usually, it is set along a boundary line such as an existing roadway. The actual burn itself is set in strips so that each successive strip runs toward that first backfire, providing each adjacent burn with no new fuel to consume."

At Raco, when a prescribed fire is scheduled, area fire division personnel turns out in force because this particular district is relatively not prone to wildfires...one fire in ten years would prove to be the norm. Prescribed burns offer valuable field experience for our men and women firefighters.

Tom Kurtz detailed the requirements for a "Prescription for Fire." He replied, "The prescription area is a block of land marked in detail on an area map. A pre-burn meeting then takes place. Firing techniques and possible fire hazards are thoroughly discussed. Weather parameters are carefully examined. The actual prescribed burn is then carefully planned and it must be perfect to be successful.

"On site, a crew constructs fire lines, often emptying natural fire breaks, then a drip torch is used to ignite narrow strips to reduce fuel.

"These measures help keep the fire from going where an unburning

Prescription for Fire

All photos courtesy of Tom Kurtz, Fire Specialist, U. S. Forest Service, Raco Station

Step 1: Setting a boundary, usually an existing roadway. A backfire will be lit here.

Step 3: A line of fire is laid with use of a drip torch

Step 2: A "nurse tanker" waiting for U.S. Forest Service pumper trucks to refill with water

Step 4: First line of fire has been set

◀ Note early spring snow cover still existing on land destined for prescribed burn

All fire personnel are U.S. Forest Service fire workers. Prescribed burn took place in the Raco District, Chippewa, or Mackinac counties.

Step 7: Burning understory growth in a pine forest; a savannah or grasslands will result, providing excellent grouse habitat.

Step 5: Crew spreads out to keep prescribed fire in proper bounds

Step 8: Backfire creates a wall of smoke as a strip of fire is put down by a drip torch

Step 6: Reindeer Moss ignites and briskly burns

area may occur. If the burn is regarded as difficult, safety zones and escape routes will be preestablished. As matters stand, lighting a prescribed fire…laying down a strip of flame…is the easiest part of the entire process.

"We tend to take every precaution possible. Pumper trucks stand by. Here at Raco, we use what we term as being a 'nurse tanker,' which we borrow from the U.S. Forest Service, Fisheries Division. The oversized tanker truck serves as a holding tank where smaller field pumper trucks can come alongside to fill up with water.

"When a trial by fire is employed, timing is critical for controlled burns to produce the results we have properly planned for."[16]

Associate Professor Roswell K. Miller, Forestry Department, Michigan Technological University, Houghton, Michigan also has vast experience with prescribed fires. Miller provided four examples of controlled burns that went wrong. First he provided a fourteen "red flag" list of situations for prescribed burning, identified by Mobley, Jackson, Balmer, Buziska, and Hough (1973). He advised that should any of the fourteen conditions listed below exist, the situation should be analyzed further before making any decision to burn:

    1: No written plan
    2: No map
    3: Heavy fuels
    4: Dry duff and soil
    5: Inadequate control lines
    6: No updated weather forecast for area
    7: Forecast does not agree with prescription
    8: Poor visibility
    9: Personnel and equipment stretched thin

10: Prescribe burning too large an area
11: Communications for all personnel not available
12: No backup plan or forces available
13: No one notified of plans to burn...adjacent property owners
14: Behavior of test fire not as prescribed[17]

Dunham Lake Fire: In May of 1975, a 640 acre prescribed fire was ignited in lower Michigan, even though the relative humidity, the only weather factor actually specified in the prescription, was far below the level prescribed. The organization was lulled into complacency because they had burned 320 acres the previous day without any problems. The Weather Bureau had forecast a Hudson Bay High Pressure weather pattern, one associated with extreme fire behavior in the Great Lakes States since at least 1964.[18] The Michigan DNR had cancelled all burning permits in the area because of the very high to extreme fire danger ratings. Strangely, adjacent landowners had not been notified of the burn ahead of time. Meanwhile, assistance from an arsonist scorched 3,500 acres more than the prescription called for and thousands of dollars worth of harvested wood was also destroyed. Sometime after the fire, a DNR official told me that, "We wouldn't notify adjacent property owners anyway; we have confidence in our prescribed burning crews." Was this more complacency?

Walsh Ditch Fire: A second example is the Walsh Ditch Fire of 1976 on the Seney National Wildlife Refuge. The refuge manager failed to recognize that a drought condition existed and when informed of it, evidently did not realize its importance in relation to the unique deep organic fuels on the refuge. When the lightning ignited fire began on or about July 30th, the refuge was already in the second stage of drought. Before the fire was extinguished, the drought had deepened almost into the fifth stage. At this time, the U.S. Fish and Wildlife Service did not have a national fire management policy or even a fire management plan for the refuge.[19]

Therefore, how could the Walsh Ditch Fire be considered a randomly ignited prescribed wilderness fire? Other "red flag" situations were present as well; condition one, no written plan; condition four, dry duff and soil;

Prescribed Fire:

- Reduces the accumulation of combustible materials

- Recycles forest nutrients

- Minimizes insect populations and spread of disease

- Encourages and maintains the growth of native trees and plants best suited to fire-adapted ecosystems

- Removes unwanted species that threaten an ecosystem's health

- Provides better access and conditions for wildlife

- Is used only under appropriate conditions and on appropriate sites

- Meets specific management objectives such as reducing wildfire potential and enhancing vegetation

- Is carefully planned in advance . . . long before ignition.

- Occurs only when optimum temperature, humidity, wind speed, and fuel moisture content occur, ensuring the fire remains inside designated boundaries and accomplishes objectives

- Is guided by smoke management plans to minimize smoke's impact on populated areas

Faces of Fire
USDA Forest Service[20]

and condition seven, forecast does not agree with prescription. How could it? There was no prescription! "Red flag" condition nine, personnel and equipment stretched too thin, also existed because the entire Seney staff was trying to put out the Pine Creek Fire which they had ignited. If we consider the Pine Creek Fire a test fire, "red flag" condition 14 was ignored because this fire certainly didn't behave as expected; it couldn't be stopped at one acre or four acres. It eventually burned 200 acres over a 56-day period.

Baraga Plains Fire: A third example was a prescribed fire in the western part of the Upper Peninsula in 1978. Three areas were to be burned in a jack pine area. The first and smallest area burned well in the morning. The second area, a larger one, showed the effects of a couple more hours of drying on the fuels and individual trees "torched out." Spot fires occurred. The largest area with the heaviest fuel load was saved until about

2:00 P.M. The results? About 450 acres got scorched instead of 100 acres prescribed. *The Daily Mining Gazette* (1978) quoted a DNR spokesman, "Conditions were ideal for the burn. There was no apparent reason for the fire to get out of control."[21] What "red flag" situations were ignored? Condition three, heavy fuels; condition 13, no one notified of plans to burn; and condition 14, behavior of test fire not as prescribed, unless we consider spotting as expected behavior.

Mack Lake Fire: My fourth and last example is the Crane Lake Prescribed Burning Unit fire for creating Kirtland's warbler habitat. This prescribed burn in lower Michigan blew up into the Mack Lake Fire in the spring of 1980. It scorched 24,700 acres of land, destroyed at least 44 structures, contributed to the death of one firefighter, and had a total cost plus loss price tag near $2.5 million. Remember standard firefighting order Number One, keep informed on fire weather conditions and forecasts? Also, remember that there are usually downdrafts under the leading edge of cold fronts? Passing cold fronts often create erratic and extreme fire behavior and frontal passage is usually followed by a wind shift? What are the chances of a cold front arriving over an area before the forecast says it will? The weather bureau had predicted a frontal movement across the state for at least two days before the burn. Did the prescription call for ignition even in light of the predictions of a frontal passage? No, the possibility of a cold front was not mentioned in the prescription. Was the prescription adequately or poorly prepared?

Professor Miller added some personal observations regarding prescribed burns, "We're professionals. Let's get our act together and do our homework! Write complete and detailed fire prescriptions. If conditions don't fit the prescription, don't ignite the fire! We must proceed more cautiously or a forester with a drip-torch may be another endangered species."[22]

The Seney Fire

High controversy surrounded the great Seney fire that scorched over 72,500 acres of federal wildland along the backbone of Michigan's Upper Peninsula.

Did a dry lightning strike begin the monstrous wildfire that dry dirt summer of 1976? Why was it not suppressed immediately instead of taking two months and the use of over a thousand men to finally lay its embers to rest?

Jack R. Frye, Service manager on the Seney National Wildlife Refuge said, "We got caught with our pants down; there is no other way you can say it." Why?

As Associate Professor Roswell Miller, Ph.D., Michigan Technological University, Forestry School, stated, "The Forest Service people would rather call it 'the late great unpleasantness' or 'the great historical and ecological event of 1976'...doublespeak at its finest."

The Seney Fire
Part 1

North Country Up In Flames...The Seney Fire

Beverly Kleikamp, author/publisher hailing from Powers, Michigan wrote one of the most accurate accounts available regarding the path of destruction taken by the Seney Fire. It was published in a short-lived publication called *Peninsula Press*, and appeared in three parts. Ms. Kleikamp's accounting sets the stage for further comment over what was done wrong and what was handled correctly with this wildfire. She presents the main cast of characters, their specific positions, and handled the assignment professionally. Her words follow:

SENEY
The Seney Fire of '76 Becomes a Part of Michigan History
By Beverly Kleikamp

Part One:

A lot was going on in Michigan in 1976. It was the centennial year, we had a new license plate, red with the white stripes of the flag, and celebrations proclaiming the "Spirit of 76" took place on the fourth of July. No one knew it that spring, but there would be another reason for 1976 being remembered in the history of years to come.

The spring fire season that year started out normal. By the end of July, however, the fire danger and drought conditions were being compared to those that preceded the historical fires in Peshtigo, Hinkly, lower Michigan and Thumb fires during 1871, 1881, and 1894 that burned millions of acres.

The normal rainfall for June through September in Marquette was 12.79 inches according to weather data records. During those months that summer, a total of 4.79 inches fell. A shortcoming of eight inches with only another half inch falling in August. These were the driest conditions since the weather stations began during 1972. By midsummer the eastern U.P. had a moisture deficiency of 9–12 inches. The Upper Peninsula became a virtual tinder box, and by midsummer there had been numerous fires reported.

When a dry thunderstorm (no rain, just thunder and lightning) passed through the Seney National Wildlife Refuge on July 30th, a bolt of lightning ignited a small fire three miles from the nearest road, and laid the groundwork for one of Michigan's most destructive and costly forest fires since 1908.

The Seney refuge in Schoolcraft County is made up of over 95,000 acres in the Great Manistique Swamp, with about one quarter of it designated as a Wilderness area where use of motorized vehicles of any kind are not allowed. Most of the refuge consists of vast open marshes and areas of rushes and sedges. Sandy ridges in these marshes support stands of mature red pine and much of the area is inaccessible on foot or otherwise.

The water table in the refuge and surrounding areas that summer had dropped by a foot. Because of the drought, the swamp and marsh vegetation on the ground had dried out along with the peat and muck soil that lay beneath it.

On August 1, a Michigan DNR fire patrol plane spotted the fire shortly after noon and radioed its location to the Seney fire station. Jack Frye, a refuge manager, was notified about 1:00 P.M. and tried to walk into the location from the Driggs River Road east of the reported fire. About a mile and a half into the timber, he ran into a dense spruce-bog thicket with high water, making it impossible to go further.

He then traveled to the C-3 Pool area and again attempted to walk into the fire area. From this direction as well, he ran into knee deep water and dense spruce thickets. This took the best part of the afternoon and it was about 5 P.M. when he again returned to the road. Mr. Frye's last contact with the DNR's aircraft indicated the fire was still about a quarter acre in size and not spreading.

The Michigan DNR was denied permission to enter the area with motorized equipment because of its status as a wilderness area, although they recommended immediate control. Mr. Frye felt there was not an emergency existing at this time that would pose a threat to the wilderness resource, human life, or damage to property, therefore no one entered the fire area. The fire continued to be monitored by refuge personnel on the ground and DNR aerial observers.

On August 2nd, the DNR's contract pilot Vern Bernard reported to Manager Frye that the fire had spread very little and was about ten acres in size. At this time the fire was still about a mile and a half from state land. From information available to Mr. Frye at this time, there was no reason to believe that the fire would not burn itself out. That, however, would soon change.

Donald Haines

Aerial view of the Seney Fire

Chapter 6
The Seney Fire

On the 3rd of August Mike Paluda, District Fire Supervisor (Newberry) from the DNR, flew over the area and now estimated the fire to be some 30–40 acres. Mr. Frye and Mechanic Zellar attempted once more to walk into the fire, this time from the south. They made it to about a mile from the fire before walking in the tangles of marsh and brush became impassible and both men became exhausted and had to turn back.

On a routine administrative flight, the Forest and Wildlife Service (FWS) aircraft arrived from Minneapolis, and a late afternoon aerial flight by Mr. Frye revealed the fire was only about a mile from state land and had grown to about 200 acres. Firefighting measures were not put into action yet because no lives or private property were threatened. The suppression of fires in a wilderness area using motorized vehicles at that time was authorized only in an emergency situation.

The situation suddenly changed on August 5th. Another fire, known as the Pine Creek fire, jumped a ditch and began expanding rapidly. Refuge Manager Frye had to commit his entire staff to this small fire from the 5th to the 17th of August along with state personnel who assisted until it was brought under control.

By August 10th it became clear that the Seney fire had now become an emergency situation. The fire had now burned 1200 acres inside the refuge. It was also known as the Walsh Ditch Fire because of the location in the refuge where it began.

Jack Frye was now advised that the southwest side of the fire must be contained to protect state land. Frye contacted Mike Paluda from the DNR who arranged to have Area Fire Supervisor George Young from Manistique and three contract bulldozers at the refuge the next morning. Things were beginning to fall into place for the forest fire that would not be forgotten in Michigan history.

Part Two:

The Seney fire continued to grow in size and was estimated at 1,600 acres on August 16, when Greg Jensen of the Boise Inter-Agency Fire center (BIFC) arrived on the scene. After flying over the fire and assessing the situation, Jensen contacted headquarters, who referred him to Region 9,

USES in Milwaukee, and made arrangements for support. There he found some manpower and equipment, but their only helicopter under contract was already committed to fighting other forest fires in Minnesota.

The BIFC personnel arrived on the 17th to take charge of fighting the fire on refuge land. John Russel took over as Federal Fire Boss and flew over the fire area to familiarize himself with the terrain. The weather was doing anything but cooperating with the efforts, as the days continued to be hot and dry with strong winds.

Two contract bulldozers and 40 men from two BIFC crews began constructing a line on the southwest flank of the fire to try and keep it from spreading into the Manistique River State Forest to the south. Two other dozers began constructing a road on the east side of Walsh Ditch, and the Hiawatha National Forest fire crew began line location and tractor construction of a fire line on the west side of Walsh Ditch to stop the fire spreading westward toward state land.

Suddenly on August 22nd the fire raged out of control. Whipped by strong northwest winds it made a nine mile run, jumped the partly completed fire lines and spread into the Manistique River State Forest, burning approximately 19,000 acres.

For the next 72 hours firefighters and other personnel worked around the clock to stop the fire's advance into the state forest. State forces joined in as they used all available manpower and equipment to establish a fire line on the southwest flank of the fire, but not before a sizable part of one of Michigan's best pine sawlog stands was blackened.

Mike Paluda, the District Fire Supervisor from Newberry, was put in charge as fire boss for the state and took immediate action. Manpower and equipment were called in from every division in the DNR and from the three regions in Michigan. It was a continuous battle to hold the fire lines as the fire continued to grow with no break in the hot, dry weather in sight.

State and Federal fire base camps were established at Cookson Bridge crossing of the Manistique River and the BIFC camp inside the refuge was evacuated. The BIFC headquarters were notified of the fire breakout and the decision was made to dispatch a Class 1 overhead fire team with Bob Webber as fire boss.

By the end of the day on the 23rd there were 35 pieces of large equipment on the fire scene. This included tractor-plows, bulldozers, tankers, pumpers and aircraft being manned by 100 DNR personnel. Even with the arrival of this equipment, it was a constant struggle to

Donald Haines

Camp scenes of the U.S. Forest Service

hold the fire lines. Any mechanical repairs had to be made on the scene by mechanics brought in from the Regional Shop along with two from the Gaylord Repair Shop.

By August 24th, Albert Livingston, Regional Forest Fire Supervisor of the DNR in Marquette reported that conditions in the U.P. were considered "explosive." The U.P. was suffering the worst drought in memory, with wells running dry and small streams becoming no more than trickles. Spot fires were cropping up in areas of the state and the Seney fire was being called the worst since '39, when a forest fire leveled thousands of acres in Presque Isle Co.

Governor Milliken declared an emergency on August 25th, allowing the Michigan National Guard to move in and become involved with the fire. $7,000 in food was being brought daily. Fifty trucks from the 107th Engineer Battalion and the 1437th Engineer Company put on over a 100,000 miles hauling personnel and equipment.

State and Federal agencies worked together against the fire that had now consumed about 20,000 acres. Help came from the private sector with aid from fire departments, fuel supplies from local oil companies, and clean drinking water hauled in milk trucks at a thousand gallons to the load. The

Schoolcraft County Road Commission helped with road and bridge repair and culvert placement, and charter buses hauled firefighters to the fire from camp.

Michigan State Police moved a Command Trailer into the fire base to coordinate emergencies, communications and highway closures. With the DNR supplying equipment and operators, and BIFC providing ground crew manpower, the work continued on constructing fire lines around a 56 mile perimeter.

The Seney fire had two unique problems to cope with, accessibility and establishing effective communication systems. The communications were often disrupted by heavy brush and trees. The terrain was a combination of peat, pools of standing water

Donald Haines

U.S. Forest Service camp

sometimes waist deep, and marsh grass, interspersed with trees, mostly jack pine, tag alder, spruce, ash and birch. Much of the land was too soft to support four-wheel drive vehicles and the fire was burning both above and below ground.

To add to the problems, on the 29th the fire jumped over the DNR line on the southeast flank and demonstrated that fire could "come alive" and "return" over previously burned marsh vegetation and organic soils. This outbreak was contained with the help of aerial water drops, but added another 15 acres to the loss.

The commands were now consolidated into joint State–Federal operations with co-fire bosses Paluda and Webber working together and making all equipment and manpower fully interchangeable. Firefighters from 22 states pressed the battle against the fire, bringing personnel numbers to above a thousand men and women on the scene.

Establishing fire lines was no easy chore, with pools of standing water, often waist deep, sprawling fields of bog and swamp that made many areas almost impossible to access. The line crews dug down to mineral soil and had to remove roots and any dead wood. Once trenches were dug, crews began backfiring a path from the trenches towards the oncoming fire using handheld flares to burn any potential fuel sources.

By August 31st, about 40,000 acres had burned. Fire lines were established and burned out around much of the fire except for the north and west flanks. After consulting with specialists and resource manager a decision was made to burn out from the north and west sides of the refuge. Plans were made for a massive backburn that would cover about 35,000 acres in hopes of containing the fire. Only one factor was needed for such an action to work...weather conditions had to be right.

Part Three:

Weather conditions did not cooperate and the scheduled backburn was held up. The fire itself only moved during daylight hours, when the conditions were dry and temperatures hot. During the night, when temps were cool and humidity higher, the fire hung back, waiting to spring again the following day.

Governor William Milliken signed a proclamation that covered all of Upper Michigan and the northern Lower Peninsula banning all outdoor burning, smoking and campfires. These were the worst fire conditions in ten years. The number of fires reported in Michigan through the first eight months of this year, 931, had already exceeded the 653 that had burned in all of 1975.

Finally on September 4th, the weather conditions were right, and the backburn began. Backfires set from the ground with the use of flame throwers, and from the air with fire grenades, all handled by skilled firefighters. Twelve crews of 20 men each, equipped with nine water tank trucks, 11 crawler tractors, and two water drop planes, worked from a seven mile front along M-28 to handle spot fires.

The weather held and the massive backburn continued along the Creighton Truck Trail and between the railroad tracks and M-28, robbing the fire of combustible fuels that remained inside the containment lines. By now more than 60,000 acres had burned, including the backburn section and over 1,000 firefighters from 29 states were involved.

Donald Haines

Clearing a fire break

On September 7th, the fire was declared "contained" with a total loss of 64,000 acres. Hopes were up and mop-up operations began, concentrating on the north, northeast and northwest sides of the fire. A Barnes infrared scanner was used to find hot spots that needed attention. Although the fire was declared contained it was not yet out.

The crews had the 64,000 acre fire surrounded with about 56 miles of fire lines and the backburn had been a success. A 250 man crew remained on the scene to carry out mop-up operations, and hundreds of the more than 1,000 federal and state firemen were sent back to their homes in the eastern, western and southern states.

Only drastic weather conditions would push the fire past the lines now, most of which had been dug with tractors. On September 12th the weather took that "drastic" turn when high winds and low humidity again created severe fire conditions.

The smoldering remains of the fire came alive again, racing across previously burned ground and formed a strong convection column. Airborne fire brands (burning debris) blew across M-28, and started two fires in the Grand Sable State Forest. One was put out after burning over 300 acres, but the other started a half mile north of the road and got away, making a seven mile overnight run that burned in excess of 5,000 acres.

The Seney fire was again declared "major" by BIFC and a General Headquarters team was brought in, commanded by Robert Sellers with Robert Compeau as the co-commander for the state. The fire effort was now divided into two zones—the new North Zone with Paluda as boss, and the old Seney Refuge Zone with Mitchel Wiles (relief for Webber) as boss.

Firefighters recently sent home were remobilized and Federal and State forces again built up to 1,000. Aerial water dropping capability was recalled with fixed wing PBY's and DC-4s, plus helicopters with buckets. Giant choppers (skycrane and chinook) were on the scene and with airforce reestablished, outbreaks were quickly doused with retardant or water-dipped from nearby ditches or lakes.

The fight was on again both from the air and on the ground. On September 15, Mike Paluda ordered a direct attack on the North Zone to hold the fire in place and try to keep it from spreading to private property to the north and east. Because of the swampy terrain much of the fire line had to be constructed by hand, with help from special equipment—a muck farm marsh plow, BLM Dragon Wagon, (a large, specialized fire truck) giant sprinkler irrigation systems, and helitack crew, all called in to cope with problems posed by this fire.

Time was not on the side of the firefighters. Stiff winds and hot weather were in the forecast. The terrain was difficult to work in, the nights cold, and to make matters worse, arsonists were in the area.

Water carrying helicopters and fixed wing PBY's dumped thousands of gallons of water on the fire with each run they made. Eight helicopters in all, three with water carrying capabilities, aided the firefighters as they worked 14 hour shifts to contain the fires both north and south of M-28.

On September 28th firefighters got a break as an afternoon long rain dampened the fire, slowing it down enough for them to complete the 32 mile containment line around the north fire. The burn was again declared "contained" and the acres now burned totaled 65,888 on the south side of the highway and 7,588 on the north side. With the final containment of the fires, many firefighters were again sent home while a small crew stayed behind to complete the mop-up operations. Even after mop-up was completed, with hot spots doused, and fire visibly out, there would still be pockets of fire that could continue to burn throughout the coming winter in the peat and muck soils of the refuge. History shows other fires in this type of soil in Southern Michigan [see Chapter 3 on bog fires] burned for years.

The Seney fire started July 30th and was finally declared contained on September 21st. During the long battle, state, federal and local fire departments, resources, and people from all over the U.S. came together in a cooperative effort to bring Michigan's worst fire since 1908 under control. The Seney fire burned 72,500 acres (112 square miles) and the final costs estimates were over $8 million.

The fire was officially declared "laid to rest" the following spring when no trace of smoldering soils could be found. During the years that have passed, new life has returned to the Seney Wildlife Refuge and the Seney Fire of 1976 has taken its place in Michigan's history.

Note: Special thanks to Gregory Lusk, Resource Protection Manager for the Upper Peninsula (DNR) for making a special trip from Marquette to their Gladstone DNR office to give me an interview. Mr. Lusk was Assistant Fire Boss for the state at the Seney Fire, and supplied me with a great deal of information. Also I would like to thank Michael Tansy, the

current Seney Refuge Manager for his help with the information on the
Seney Fire. (Bev Kleikamp)[23]

Questions…Questions…Always Questions

During and following the infamous Seney Fire (Walsh Ditch Fire),
questions arose time and time again from fire researchers across the nation.

Roswell Miller, Associate Professor of Forestry, Michigan Technological
University, Houghton, Michigan wrote the following statement regarding
the Seney blaze in an unpublished professional paper titled, "Yellowstone—
Background and Synopsis of the Yellowstone Fires of 1988."

1976–Was the second year of a two-year drought in much of the U.S. and
the drought included the upper midwest. The Walsh Ditch (Seney National
Wildlife Refuge) fire burned between July and November, and contained
72,500 acres inside the final control lines. Due to mismanagement by the
U.S. Fish and Wildlife Service, the fire also crossed out of the wilderness
area (where it started) and out of the refuge onto other State and National
Forest lands in Michigan. The Seney fire produced some of the first lessons
with 'natural fires in designated wilderness areas' for the Department of the
Interior. In the absence of a prescription, in the absence of the ability to
monitor the fire, in the absence of a decision maker with fire management
training or experience, in the presence of a unique weather situation
(drought), and in the presence of a unique fuel situation (extremely dry
organic soils), the fire should never have been allowed to burn, and eventually cost eight million dollars to suppress. There is little argument about the
positive ecological effect of the Seney fire on the ecosystem. There is also
little argument on the social effect—nobody used the wilderness area
before the fire, and nobody has used the area since (It's a scuddzy piece of
real estate that only the wildlife and mosquitoes could use).

1977—At least one National Park (Isle Royale) had a fire management plan, which included, among other things, a prescription which recognized a buffer zone within (rather than outside of) the designated wilderness area; a prescription which recognized such fire behavior variables as temperature, relative humidity, wind speed, fuel moisture, and the burning index; and allowed natural fires to be suppressed under conditions of drought, dangerous synoptic weather patterns, in case of multiple fires, or in case personnel to monitor and suppress the fire(s) were not available.
Note: Dr. Miller wrote the prescription for the Park Service, Isle Royale

The rest of the paper mainly dealt with the Yellowstone fire, which has in essence helped shape the future of wilderness fires today. Wildfires allowed to freely burn brought about cries of outrage from Americans all across the country.

In his Yellowstone paper, Dr. Miller points out a need for change after the burnings of the Seney Refuge and Yellowstone. His words follow:

It's too bad the Yellowstone fires of 1988 had to happen before land managers sat up and took notice of the things fire management specialists had been saying for years. If we review the natural fire policy of the Park Service, we can see that it could be ecologically and physically possible. It can also be economically efficient, socially and culturally acceptable, and administratively practical. Therefore, though we might agree that the policy is a good one, even though we might also agree that a little more man-planned prescribed fire might be a better answer to an obvious fuels management problem, even in designated wilderness areas and national parks, the policy itself was not the problem.

The real problem, in the Yellowstone fire situation this past year, was in the administration of the policy. Yes, we might even agree that its administration was ecologically and physically possible. But does a 112 million dollar suppression bill sound like an economic necessity? Certainly the public and professional outcry against the "destruction" of close to half of our oldest National Park would seem to suggest that the administration of that policy was not socially or culturally acceptable. Finally, given the administrative blunders made in the past twelve to sixteen years, I have my doubts as to the administrative practicality of administering such a policy.

Don't government agencies learn from their sister agencies? Don't they heed the words of their own Chief of Fire Management? Don't they recognize extreme fuel, weather and multiple ignition situations when they occur? Have they lost sight of the fact that the natural fire policy is a guide to the management of fires in wilderness areas rather than a reason to neglect them, even if the fires should be allowed to burn, given the fuel and weather situation which prevailed? It will be interesting to see what changes may eventually come from all of this. If this had occurred to anyone other than a government agency, someone would be looking for a new job.[24] ...end of Dr. Miller's report.

Donald Haines

A backfire was set adjacent to this ditch

In his Yellowstone paper, Dr. Miller made reference to some of the things we should have learned during the 1976 Walsh Ditch Fire at Seney, but subsequently didn't. He also commented, "I guess I believe that more Seneys will occur, more Mack Lakes will occur, and more Yellowstones will also occur."

Luke Popovich wrote a stirring article titled, "U.P. In Flames...Taking Heat On the Seney" that appeared in the March 1997 issue of the ***Journal*** *of Forestry* appearing in a section known as "Forestry Today."

Mr. Popovich asks some hard questions:

For while you (Jack R. Frye, Service Manager on the Seney National Wildlife Refuge) watched, studied your regulations, and consulted your superiors, the remote wildfire (Walsh Ditch Fire) of little consequence mushroomed into an $8 million blaze. By the time you were authorized to act, the fire would sweep through 55,000 acres of the Seney, 15,800 acres of the adjacent Manistique State Forest, and 1,500 acres of private land. The governor had to call out the National Guard. Hundreds of federal firefighters were flown in from as far away as Idaho and North Carolina in an exercise that reminded a few veterans of their days on Iwo Jima. State officials threatened to sue the federal government for damages. And you, if you were the refuge manager, would become a local antihero.

Why did a fire, which could have been extinguished by a score of men in several days, require a thousand men and over two months to put out?...

If a federal fire poses a threat to state lands, at what point does the manager cave in to the state?

As the smoke filled his nostrils, it was a question that Frye pondered, too. Besides, he knew that if the state clamored for action, as it was soon to do, he could not spend money on a costly fire fight. The money spent monitoring the fire the first week was coming from his regular operating budget. At that rate, he noted, 'I'd be broke in three days.' The reason is simple: The Fish and Wildlife Service has no access to fire suppression fund. 'The Director has to go hat in hand to Congress and beg for money,' remarked one Service official.

One DNR official remarked that if the Fish and Wildlife Service needed a proving ground for their particular type of fire management, where else could they possibly locate a better target than say, the Upper Peninsula of Michigan, where 72,000 acres actually burned without a single serious injury, never threatened a town or village, and where its former land use so quickly returned to its former state.

Other questions that crossed my mind over the entire Seney Fire situation were:

1) Why did a National Wildlife Refuge manager prescribe a fire, minus a written prescription, during a severely dry season, and when only six people worked under his command?

2) Was this manager so untrained and unskilled that he felt no need to listen to a Michigan DNR fire specialist advising him that conditions were not favorable for a prescribed burn?

3) Why was the Walsh Ditch Fire not suppressed when it was merely ¼ acre in size when spotted by a DNR air patrol? Before it was squelched months later, this pint-sized fire burned over 110 square miles. This fire ran unchecked for three weeks.

4) Why were bureaucrats so slow in freeing up funds and men to fight this major blaze?

5) Why were communications so poor during the height of suppression attempts that helicopters water-bombing the fire, misdirected their cargo dropping the bombs in one instance on the purposely set backfire?

6) Why did it take from July 7 to August 31 to finally put the prescribed Pine Creek burn out?

Questions will always persist. Our hope is that history will not repeat itself.[25]

A Scientific Research Paper Continues the Controversy

A paper was presented at the Fifth Joint Conference on Fire and Forest Meteorology sponsored by the American Meteorological Society and the Society of American Foresters, March 14–16, 1978 at Atlantic City, New Jersey. That paper, which details in part the Seney Fire, or Walsh Ditch Fire, as it is also known, was written by Roswell K. Miller, Associate Professor of Forestry, Michigan Technological University, Houghton, Michigan. It is included in its entirety, for to better understand the problems presented at Seney, one must bear some knowledge of the accompanying Drought Index.

The Keetch–Bryam Drought Index and Three Fires in Upper Michigan, 1976
Roswell K. Miller, Associate Professor of Forestry
Michigan Technological University, Houghton, Michigan

The Upper Peninsula of Michigan encompasses approximately nine million acres of commercial forest land, and another million acres of non-commercial forests and swamps, lakes and streams, cities, towns and farms. Included within its borders are two national forests, a national park, a national lakeshore, a national wildlife refuge, fifteen state forests, seven-teen state parks and four small Indian reservations.

The Upper Peninsula is noted for Longfellow's "Song of Hiawatha," copper and iron mining, lumber and pulpwood production, the "Soo" locks, the Mackinac Bridge, the Lake Superior shoreline, Michigan Technological University, an unbelievable snowfall in the winter, and the Walsh Ditch Fire. Four places named in this paper include a small area on the south-western tip of Isle Royale National Park, the City of Houghton which is sixty to sixty-five miles south of Isle Royale, a much larger area in the eastern Upper Peninsula closely identified with the Seney National Wildlife

Refuge, and the City of Newberry which is about twenty-five miles east of the Seney area.

1: Drought History

Data published by Strommen, et.al. (1969) indicate that major droughts have occurred in the Upper Peninsula in the recent past. These occurred in 1930 and 1931, 1933 and 1934, and 1936 and 1937 when over 26,000 acres or 19 percent of the land area of Isle Royale burned. Major droughts have also occurred in 1940 and 1941, 1947 and 1948, 1955 in the east half, 1957 in the west half, 1963 and 1964, and 1967.

The most recent drought, which occurred in 1975 and 1976, has been called the hardest drought to hit the Upper Peninsula in over 100 years. All of these droughts, plus many lesser ones, have been documented from weather records using the meteorological drought index developed by Palmer (1965).

The Drought Index (DI) developed by Keetch and Byram (1968) will be used throughout the remainder of this paper instead of the Palmer Index for three reasons. First the Keetch–Byram

Donald Haines

A U.S. Forest Service worker measures the depth of dry earth

DI can be easily calculated by the personnel located at various field stations that are most concerned with weather changes, fire danger, and fire management on a daily basis. Second, this DI can easily be updated on a daily basis to provide a continuous record which is compatible with the other indices of the National Fire Danger Rating System (NFDRS) developed by Deeming, et al. (1974). And third, this DI does provide an index, based upon the observations at a single weather station, for localized conditions which are very important in day-to-day fire management decisions (Haines, et al., 1976).

The Keetch–Byram DI is one that was developed especially for fire control purposes. The DI itself is a number which can meaningfully be translated directly into the number of inches of cumulative moisture deficiency in deep duff or organic soil layers by moving the decimal point two places to the left. I have done this in the rest of this paper. This DI was specifically designed to represent the net effect of both evapotranspiration and precipitation on the flammability of organic material in the ground. Put another way, this DI represents the deep drying or organic soils, peats and mucks, which occurs during prolonged drought. Although closely related, the DI does not measure the same thing as either the energy release component of the NFDRS or the buildup index of former fire danger rating methods, two measures which are used primarily to indicate the drying of large, dead surface fuels.

Continuous weather observations taken at the Department of Forestry in Houghton show that the four years, 1971 through 1974, had relatively normal summers and fire seasons. The six month periods between May and October of each year produced precipitation which was fairly well distributed throughout each

Donald Haines

Camp scene of the U.S. Forest Service

summer. Respectively, 14, 21, and 15 inches of total rainfall occurred. The average DI during these four summers stayed below 1.75" in only the first stage of drought.

In 1975, a year with less than 14 inches of precipitation during the same six month period, a dry spell began in mid-July and continued. By August 12th, the Houghton area was into the fourth stage of drought. The DI eventually reached a cumulative moisture deficiency of 4.27" in September before relief occurred in the form of precipitation. Nor was the drought broken, that is, reduced to less than 2.00", until October 23rd.

In 1976, the DI climbed relatively steadily from May 1st to July 8th, dropped slightly, climbed even higher from July 13th to August 9th, was temporarily reduced again, and then increased to the fourth stage of drought. This lasted until September 18th when rainfall again reduced it somewhat. The summer of 1976 was one in which our weather station recorded only 7.7 inches of precipitation for the May through October period. At the end of October, the DI was still in the second stage of drought with 2.28" of cumulative moisture deficiency.

Weather data taken at the headquarters of the Seney National Wildlife Refuge show that 1976 was the second consecutive year that they also experienced deep drought conditions. The DI began climbing as soon as the snow was gone in May and was into the second stage of drought by June 25th. They received some rain on July 14th, but the DI had increased to the second stage again by July 22nd. The DI continued to climb until it reached a peak of 4.87" of cumulative moisture deficiency on October 4th, and remained in the fourth stage of drought until October 14th, finally dropping back into the second stage of drought on October 22nd.

2: Agencies and Their Fire Policies

Before giving a chronological history of three fires which burned in the Upper Peninsula between the dates of July 7th and October 31st, 1976, some further data is necessary in order to understand the scenario and its participants.

The National Park Service (NPS) of the U.S. Department of the Interior administers Isle Royale National Park. The NPS has a history of fire management which includes the use of prescribed fire, both natural and man-caused, in the Sequoia and Kings Canyon Parks, the Grand Teton Park, Yellowstone Park, and others.

Currently, the general fire management policy of the NPS allows "*some*" natural (lightning-caused) fires to burn; when they help reach management objectives; when they do not threaten human life; when they do not threaten developed properties; when they *not threaten properties outside the boundaries of the unit* and when they burn only *under specific prescribed conditions.*" [emphasis added].

The Isle Royale National Park staff switched to the use of the NFDRS at the start of its fire management program to include both natural and man-set prescribed fires in an attempt to return fire to its natural role in the environment of the island wilderness. The bulk of the 200 island park, about 90% of its 133,844 acres, is destined to be added to our national wilderness system. The soils on the island include duff layers up to about one foot thick, but there are no extensive peat or muck areas. The weather is, of course, greatly influenced by Lake Superior.

The Fish and Wildlife Service (FWS) of the U.S. Department of the Interior administers the Seney National Wildlife Refuge. The Seney Refuge is a 95,455 acre tract, primarily consisting of bogs and wetlands. Of this total, 25,150 acres have already been designated as wilderness. The FWS currently has no fire management program.

The fire suppression policies in 1976 were to: (1) Extinguish wild fires using any available means. Keep fire damage to a minimum and at a reasonable suppression cost to the agency. (2) For wilderness fires—similar to the above except that equipment is authorized to fight a wilderness fire *only in a recognized emergency situation.* (3) For prescribed fire-use as a management tool *under careful regulation.*" [emphasis added].

In 1976 the Seney Refuge had not had a fire for the past five years, its manager was not experienced in fire suppression work, its fire plan had not been updated since part of the refuge had been designated as wilderness, and it was still not using the NFDRS. The refuge was known to contain an extensive area of peat soils, up to eight or more feet deep, and lightning fires had occurred in the peat areas in 1954, 1964 and 1967.

Chapter 6
The Seney Fire

The Forest Fire Division of the Michigan Department of Natural Resources (DNR) is charged with the protection from fire of all state and private lands in Michigan. Because of the interspersed pattern of land ownership within the state, every fire is considered a wildfire unless it is a purposely set prescribed fire. Because of the inherent capricious nature of fire behavior, the DNR essentially follows a fire policy of "when in doubt, put it out." In 1976 the DNR was a partner with the FWS in a cooperative fire control agreement whereby these agencies would help each other in case of a fire emergency.

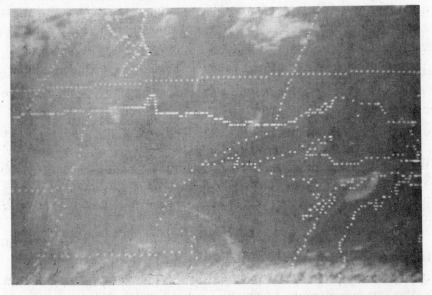

Donald Haines

Satellite view of the Seney Fire (known as the Walsh Ditch Fire by U.S. Foresters)

The DNR has used the NFDRS since 1972 and currently keys the manning levels for their forest fire field offices to both the Ignition Component and the Burning Index of the NFDRS. The technicians, fire supervisors and fire control specialists of the DNR are all well experienced in the suppression of fires, including peat and muck fires in the areas where these organic soils exist.

3: Fire Chronology

July 7, 1976: The Pine Creek "Prescribed Burn" is started by FWS personnel on Seney Refuge lands. No written prescription is available. The plan is to burn 40 acres, but the DNR, knowing the area and expecting trouble, convinces the refuge staff to try burning only one acre first, as a test fire. The DNR points out the drought conditions in their advice to the FWS. There has been only 1.44" of effective precipitation since May 17th (effective precipitation is any amount over 0.2" being considered intercepted by vegetation and not reaching the soil surface.) Although calculated *ex post facto*, the DI for the Seney Headquarters weather station is already at 2.52" of cumulative moisture deficiency, more than halfway through the second stage of drought.

July 30: A thunderstorm passes over the designated wilderness area of the Seney Refuge, igniting what is now known as the Walsh Ditch Fire. The DI is now at 2.61".

August 3: The Pine Creek Fire, thought to be contained at one acre, 27 days ago, is now 5 acres in size and is still being suppressed by FWS personnel. The DI has climbed to 2.86" and the Walsh Ditch Fire, with no suppression action being taken on it, has grown to an estimated 200 acres. At Newberry, the 2:00 P.M. Eastern Daylight Time, relative humidity is 28% and the fine fuel moisture has dropped to 87.

August 6: The entire refuge staff of six is working to contain the Pine Creek Fire which started growing rapidly the day before. The DI is 3.04" in the third stage of drought. Meanwhile, approximately 180 miles to the northwest on Isle Royale, the Card Point Fire, apparently started by lightning within the wilderness portion of the park, is now reported as being only 100 square feet in size.

August 11: With the Walsh Ditch Fire now estimated to be over 1200 acres, the Pine Creek "Prescribed Burn" is finally contained at 200 acres through the combined effort of FWS and DNR crews. The DI has climbed to 3.42" and no suppression action is yet being taken on the Walsh Ditch Fire. It is still burning within the designated wilderness boundary of the Seney Refuge.

August 18: The Card Point Fire on Isle Royale is spreading, in the absence of control action, and is now over 1/10 acres in size, twelve days after it started. The DI at Seney is 3.49" and DNR crews are finally allowed to begin suppression effort on the Walsh Ditch Fire—now 1800 acres in size. The Boise Interagency Fire Center (BIFC) in Idaho is in charge of the fire and is directing the mobilization and suppression efforts of DNR and federal fire crews.

August 23: The Walsh Ditch Fire runs nine miles to the southeast, aided by relatively warm temperatures and fairly low humidities. Strong winds from the northwest push it over partially completed fire lines, out of the Seney Refuge, and onto State Forest lands. There are 35 pieces of equipment and 100 men committed to the fire, but the next day it will have grown to around 20,000 acres as the DI continues to climb over 3.9". At Newberry, at 2:00 P.M., the relative humidity was 38% and the fine fuel moisture was down to 8% again.

August 27: Manpower committed to the Walsh Ditch Fire now exceeds 1000, having been drawn from 29 states, including Alaska, with support coming from the National Guard, the State Police, County Highway Departments, School Districts and other units.

August 28: The DI is over 4.1", the fire again jumps lines on the southeast flank, reburning over previously burned areas.

August 29: An infrared scanner maps the fire from the air and it has grown to 30,850 acres. On Isle Royale, however, the Card Point Fire is still less than 2.3 acres in size and is still being monitored, not suppressed, by NPS staff.

August 31: Lines are well established and burned out around the Walsh Ditch Fire now, except for the north and west sides. The decision is made to burn-out the remainder of the wilderness area rather than to fight the fire within it. Approximately 35,000 more acres will thus be added to the already 40,000 acres burned. The Pine Creek "Prescribed Burn" is finally declared out, after a small river had been diverted by bulldozers to completely drown the fire. The DI is now at 4.19" and fire crews are waiting for

Donald Haines

Aerial view of a U.S. Forest Service camp

favorable weather conditions to conduct the burn-out. At Newberry, 2:00 P.M. weather shows a relative humidity of 84%, wind out of the northeast at 3 mph, and a fine fuel moisture of 20%. Mop-up is continuing on the south and east sides of the fire.

September 3: Newberry reports 2:00 P.M. winds out of the south at 20 mph. The relative humidity is down to 41% and the fine fuel moisture is down to 10%. The Walsh Ditch Fire makes a run to the north towards State Highway M-28, the only hardtop road between the fire and Lake Superior. The DI for Seney is now at 4.25" and the fire reaches 49,000 acres. The next day, burning-out will be tried along M-28, even though conditions may not be good.

September 7: The Walsh Ditch Fire is declared contained. Burning-out operations have been partly successful. Two slight rains, totaling .31 inches since the first of the month have helped. Fire size is now listed at 64,000 acres, the largest in Michigan since 1908. Demobilization of the manpower and equipment begins and mop-up continues. The DI is now 4.4" and still rising.

September 12: The DI is now at 4.67". The 2:00 P.M. weather at Newberry shows a relative humidity of 28%, fine fuel moisture at 5%, wind out of the south at 10 mph and a relatively high energy release component of 19. The fire comes alive again, returns previously burned areas, forms a convection column, and two spot fires are started north of M-28. One is contained, the other makes a seven mile overnight run to the north on State Forest land on a one-mile-wide front. A new BIFC fire overhead team is brought in on the 13th, water bombers and helicopters are recalled to the fire, manpower is again boosted up to 1000, and the fire is estimated at 64,000 acres.

September 18: With the Walsh Ditch Fire now shown to be 72,500 acres, an arsonist sets a fire 15 miles south of Seney in a Jack Pine stand in the Hiawatha National Forest. Men and equipment are dispatched from the Seney Fire and they hold the new fire to 300 acres, even though it "crowns out." The DI at Seney is now 4.64". Newberry's 2:00 P.M. weather shows a relative humidity of 32%, a fine fuel moisture of 6% and wind from the west at 8 mph.

September 21: Seney's .24 inches of rain and the completion of the fireline around the breakout north of M-28 allow the fire to be declared contained again. Mop-up continues around an 88-mile perimeter containing 72,500 acres. The DI is 4.66" and still climbing. Meanwhile, on Isle Royale, the Card Point Fire is now over 3 acres in size and still being watched by NPS staff.

October 4: The DI at Seney reaches its high of 4.87" in the fourth stage of drought.

October 5: A rain at Seney last night dropped 1.09 inches of water on the parched land. The DI is now down to 4.01" of cumulative moisture deficiency.

October 10: Seney temperatures dropped last night to 31°F. and produced the first light frost of the fall.

October 16: The first snowfall of the season covers the refuge with an inch of wet snow. The DI is still in the third stage of drought at 3.63". The Walsh Ditch Fire is still listed as contained—not controlled, not out. The Seney Fire Evaluation Team of the FWS begins its work within the fire area.

October 18: In preparation for closing down the island park, a crew of NFS personnel begin the suppression of the Card Point Fire.

October 25: The DI at Seney is now down to 2.78". On Isle Royale, the Card Point Fire is given its final mop-up and declared out.

October 31: DI calculations were terminated for the Seney weather station at 2.78".

Sometime during the winter of 1976–77, the Walsh Ditch Fire was officially declared out. The exact date is unimportant. Winter rains and snows caused water levels to rise in the peat bogs and finally put it out.

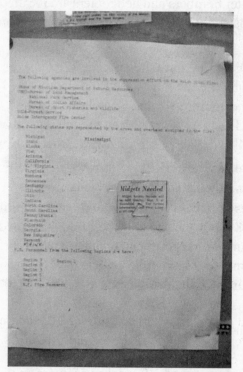

Donald Haines

Work order—personnel assignments posted for the firefighting crew

4. Summary:

The Card Point Fire burned from August 6th until October 25th, consuming a total of 5 acres in 80 days. It can be considered a "pre-scribed natural wilderness fire" which met management objectives. No unusual fuel situation existed, no unusual weather situation existed, and only 69 man-hours were spent in its eventual suppression. The DI on the west end of Isle Royale only climbed to 3.04" all summer. This fire will remain only as a small scar within a wilderness area, as an addition to the fire statistics of Isle Royale National Park, and as a four-page report in the files of the NPS.

The Pine Creek Fire burned from July 7th until August 31st. It was a purposely set "prescribed fire," set without a written prescription or fire management policy, which was supposed to burn one, or perhaps, forty acres. It eventually consumed 200 acres in 56 days. The fire could not be controlled because of the combination of an unusual drought and an un-usual fuel situation. Even though hundreds of man hours and equipment-hours were spent on its eventual control, the lessons learned from this fire will probably soon be forgotten, overwhelmed by the magnitude of what happened a few miles away.

The Walsh Ditch Fire burned from July 30th at least until late October. It was a naturally set wilderness wildfire, allowed to burn without the monitoring which would be called for under a rational wilderness fire management policy and plan, while people argued over who might pay the suppression costs and whether or not the fire would "behave itself" and meet nebulous unwritten management objectives. It had grown to 1800 acres before suppression effort was initiated, although permission to sup-press it was sought by DNR personnel who were experienced in fighting fires burning in similar unusual fuel and weather situations. However, nobody was calculating a drought index to help back up this request to start suppression.

Over 90 days later, the fire had covered 72,500 acres (over 110 square miles), although within its perimeter lie 25 square miles of unburned areas. The suppression costs alone, not including losses to adjacent state and private land, are expected to exceed eight million dollars, making this the second most expensive fire in the history of the United States. Preliminary investigations reveal that the ecological effect of the fire within the Seney Refuge and its wilderness area are probably quite positive. The effects on state and private lands burned outside the refuge are certainly negative. The teamwork and cooperation of both federal and state fire overhead and crews on such a large fire was also a demonstration of the capacity of people to work together toward a common goal. The Walsh Ditch Fire is probably the only one of these three fires that will "go down" in the history books.

What are the lessons we have learned, or relearned, or should have learned, from these three fires? First, I think more than ever that we now know that peat and muck soils are special wildland fire fuels whose burning characteristics must be appraised differently from any other natural fuel.

Second, I think that we should recognize the value of a drought index, such as the one developed by Keetch and Byram, in the appraisal of the burning characteristics of peat and muck fuels. Regardless of the level of any of the daily fire danger indices contained within the NFDRS. These organic soils, when dry enough, will burn and continue to burn and resist control efforts more tenaciously than any other wildland fuel, because of this, any fire in organic soil becomes a threat as an ignition source for surface fires if and when daily burning conditions become favorable.

Third, I hope we've learned our lesson concerning the difference between a naturally started wildfire and a naturally started prescribed fire, whether in a designated wilderness area or not. In the absence of a fire management policy and plan, in the absence of a precise prescription for allowing a fire to burn within a wilderness area, without the ability to adequately monitor a fire and have well trained fire management personnel assess its potential threat, and with a unique fuel situation affected by an even more unique weather situation, any fire should be considered a wildfire and action should be taken to suppress it immediately. We certainly cannot afford to make any more 7¼ to 8 million dollar mistakes. To do so surely threatens any advances we may have made in the area of fire management in the past few years.

Plans are currently progressing to add a 1000-hour time-lag fuel-moisture index to the NFDRS (Deeming, 1976). Whether or not this additional index will adequately appraise the potential threat of deep peat fuels under long term drought conditions remains to be seen. I suggest that the Keetch–Byram DI should be used if peat fuels are present within the boundaries of a protection district, if drought is suspected, and until we can correlate the 1000-hour index with the DI. A Keetch–Byram DI value greater than 2.00" of cumulative moisture deficiency certainly warrants a very cautious appraisal of the burning potential of deep peat fuels.[26]

Has the National Guard Been a Contributing Factor in Fire Situations Near Grayling?

An ongoing controversy between the military and citizens in the Grayling area has continued for years. The question: Have the National Guard training units contributed to fires on lands surrounding the base?

*Vocal advocates for the people have included the AuSable Manistee Action Council, the Anglers of the AuSable, and the venerable champion of environmental common sense, Glen Sheppard of the **North Woods Call**.*

Has the National Guard Been a Contributing Factor in Fire Situations Near Grayling?

Citizens Speak Out Against the Guard

In a letter, Ron Schwarz of Waters, Michigan describes a recent fire that affected him and his family:

Lack of spring rains put the forest fire hazards in the woods around our home in the Gaylord area into the very high and extremely dangerous status. No outdoor burning warnings had already been enacted by the DNR. By June 12th the conditions were listed as explosive. *The News Daily* reported grass fires and outdoor smoking precautions. There was much talk of prohibiting the Fourth of July fireworks display and campfires at the State Parks. The woods were dry; very, very, very dry....No rain in the forecast.

My wife and I were in horror when the National Guard started firing artillery Saturday, June 13, 1992. This should not have been allowed because of the fires artillery firing creates.

On Monday, June 15th at 11:30 A.M. my neighbor, Dr. Gary Jenks phoned me at work to look at the smoke cloud rising from the Range 40 area—which is just south of our homes on Section One and Guthrie Lakes. He asked me if I knew of any fire reports. I called the DNR. They told me the military had a fire going but had it contained. I called Camp Grayling Fire Dept. Captain Arndt said the fire barn was empty, so they must be out somewhere. He would find out and call me back. Captain Arndt called at 12:15 and said, "Yeah, they got a fire going on North Camp Range 40 and they were rolling everything they got."

The smoke was now reaching my shop (Waters Garage), six miles east. I called the DNR again and I was told the military had the fires under control and they were contained in the impact area. I questioned the wind direction being southeast; it posed a danger to my home and he said, "Yeah, that's something to watch."

Chapter 7
Has the National Guard Been a Contributing Factor in Fire Situations Near Grayling?

Smoke hung in the air everywhere. The local fire department was sent out to look for fire on I-75. The DNR spotter plane was also sent up. This was about 5:00 P.M. When my wife got home, she found the house and the surrounding woods filled with heavy smoke and called me to investigate on my way home.

At the corner of my private road and the power line road, I encountered much smoke and saw a National Guard fire truck ahead of me. I turned left and went up the power line to get a better view of the threatening situation.

Ron Schwarz

Mothers Day Fire, 1992—"More Water"

I was sure the fire had crossed the range berm and was in the area around my home. From the top of Redner Hill (¼ mile from my road) I saw a fire truck at the bottom and pulled alongside to question the men in the cab who appeared to be resting. I asked, "Is everything under control?" The driver replied, "Ha, in the military nothing is ever under control!"

Ron Schwarz

Road to Ron Schwarz's home is free of smoke after the fire is out; photo taken June 18, 1992, 11:00 A.M.

I was not impressed and he remarked that neither was he. He said he had been in smoke all day and if I wanted to talk to the man in charge he's right over there...poking his thumb over his right shoulder. I asked if it was Capt. Hanson, the Ranger Officer, but he replied, "No, it is General Mathews."

I drove about 200 feet east along the impact fence to a man in field gear resting his arms on the fence wire watching the ground fire in front of him. "General?" I said as I exited my truck. He turned and I shook his hand introducing myself. He said he had heard of me before. I asked why the fire wasn't being put out and why the DNR wasn't called in. He said that it was a necessary part of training and once it all burned there would be nothing left to burn. I disagreed. Due to the wind conditions it could easily cross the berm and threaten my house. He assured me they had it under control. I informed him that the man in the fire truck said nothing was under control. At this time, Colonel Koppa appeared and asked me if it was my time to be here. He said, "Ron, you know what I mean."

I said, "OK, I'll just leave." I backed up my truck and drove up the hill where I encountered my wife.

Has the National Guard Been a Contributing Factor in Fire Situations Near Grayling?

We drove home. Smoke was getting thicker and we were scared! I called the news station and many of our neighbors. My wife went back to talk to the General. The news (WUPTV Channel 9 & 10) said they would meet us at the Water s Exit of I-75 at 8:15 P.M. It was now 7:00 P.M. My wife returned disgusted with the General's lack of response, and we began laying out water hoses. About twenty-five people living on the lake came to my house to interview with newsman Eric Fletcher.

Many of them escorted Eric to Redner Hill where a video tape was made. The military had left the scene.

The fires continued, the artillery firing continued, and the smoke spread through the woods, from the southeasterly winds for two more days. The DNR finally called a cease fire on Wednesday, July 17th afternoon, and the National Guard complied.

The only good thing that came of this was that our house was still standing and life goes on. Ronald Schwarz Waters, MI[27]

There were others who openly complained about the above described incident. Following local TV coverage, residents responded through "Letters to the Editor" pages of local newspapers. Headlines of area newspapers screamed:

Ron Schwarz

Road to Ron Schwarz's home is full of smoke; photo taken June 15, 1992, 11:00 A.M.

Prospects For Forest Fires Are 'Very High'

Guard Catches Heat For Fires, Admits Problems

State, Forest Service Playing With Fire, Official Says

Northern Michigan A Tinder Box—Firefighter Shortage

Fire Consumes 20 Dwellings

Fires, Noise, Litter Anger Camp Neighbors

Gleaning fire-related paragraphs printed in some of the above headlined articles illustrates the mindset of the general population during the dry season that occurred that spring and summer of 1992:

The Detroit News: June 25, 1992

Northern Michigan A Tinderbox—Firefighter Shortage
DNR warns a blaze in mature forests could burn across the state

...A 700-acre fire earlier this month destroyed 19 homes in Oscoda County (Luzerne area) before being extinguished by heavy rains.

The DNR has 96 fire officers to guard 20 million acres of state forest land. That's down from 180 two decades ago and many of the 50 fire stations are not staffed, said Art Sutton, a leader in the DNR's resource protection unit.

...The need for more fire officers became clear last week when a fire broke out in a national forest near Luzerne, said Scott Heather, a DNR field supervisor in Roscommon.

The fire blackened 700 acres as state and U.S. Forest Service crews fought it. When a fire ignited six miles to the west in a state forest, there weren't enough crews to handle it, Heather said. "And we had areas to the south that were left unprotected."[28]

⌧ ⌧ ⌧ ⌧ ⌧

**Has the National Guard Been a Contributing Factor
in Fire Situations Near Grayling?**

The Bay City Times: May 7, 1992
Prospects For Forest Fires Are 'Very High'

Officials have canceled weekend burning permits across northern
Michigan and alerted firefighters as warm, breezy weather threatened an
outbreak of forest fires.

"Early May historically is peak fire season," said Greg Lusk, assistant
regional forest manager for DNR's Marquette office.

...Firefighters across lower Michigan have been put on alert in case
they are needed to help with large blazes, said Duane Brooks, a DNR fire
official posted in the AuSable State Forest.[29]

☒　☒　☒　☒　☒

Crawford County Avalanche: May 7, 1992
DNR Recommends Recycling Over Burning Yard Waste

The above headlines accompanied an article telling homeowners to mulch
their yard wastes or compost them over burning due to the high fire danger
in the immediate area. The same issue of the *Avalanche* also held a sidebar
affording "Range Firing" as follows:

Range Firing

Range firing will be conducted at Camp Grayling in the following areas:

The Small Arms ranges located west of Lake Margrethe, north of
Howe Road, east of the gas pipeline, and south of Portage Creek. Firing
will begin on May 8 and cease on May 10.

The Small Arms ranges located at Arrowhead Road in Kalkaska
County. Firing will begin on May 8 and cease on May 10.

Range 30 Complex located north of North Down River Road, east of
Jones Lake Road, south of County Road 612 and west of Damon Truck
Trail. Firing will begin on May 8 and cease May 10.

The Range 40 Complex, located north of County Road 612, east of Guthrie Lake, south of Old State Road. 618, and west of County Rd. P97 (Twin Bridge Rd). Firing will begin on May 8, cease on May 13.

The Range 40 Complex, Air to Ground, located north of County Rd. 612, east of Guthrie Lake, south of Old State Rd., 618, and west of County Rd. F-97 (Twin Bridge Rd). Firing will be from May 8 through May 9, and May 12 through May 13.[30]

☒   ☒   ☒   ☒   ☒

It was no small wonder the citizenry was nervous; on one hand the Michigan DNR issues no-burning directives, yet the Guard continues incendiary operations.

On June 12, 1992 Gary Boushelle, Acting Deputy Director of the Michigan DNR, Region II Headquarters at Roscommon, Michigan, sent a letter reprinted on page 91.

The issue at that time, was more or less resolved with the issuance of a media press release explaining the position of the National Guard, Grayling, Michigan. A copy of that press release follows:

May 29, 1992

Regional Chiefs Examine Fire Controls

Regional heads of the Departments of Natural Resources and Military Affairs met last week to review fire control measures employed during the mid-June fires on Camp Grayling's range impact areas.

The following information is provided, according to Camp Grayling's commander, Lieutenant Colonel Wayne Koppa, both to answer citizen concerns, and to clarify issues related to the fires of June 14–17 within the fenced-off range areas of Camp Grayling.

"DNR and DMA have worked extensively over the last few years on

Chapter 7
Has the National Guard Been a Contributing Factor in Fire Situations Near Grayling?

Region II Headquarters
P.O. Box 128
Roscommon, Michigan 48653
June 12, 1992
Lt. Col. Wayne Koppa
Camp Commander
Camp Grayling, Michigan 49739-0001

Dear Lt. Col. Koppa:

Pursuant to the Mutual Aid Agreement between the Michigan Department of Natural Resources and the Michigan Department of Military Affairs, I request that the following actions be taken to prevent forest fires: employee risk-reduction measures necessary to minimize the incidence of fires that would result from training and/or ammunition use.

I formally request that you immediately stop the use of all pyrotechnics until further notice when conditions become favorable for their use.

The Grayling area is experiencing very dry conditions. Only 0.23 of an inch of rain was recorded at our Grayling weather station since the first of May. Over the past five weeks an average of 50 fires per week have been responded as conditions continue to worsen.

I am very appreciative of the care and concern you have shown this spring and early summer. I understand that you have already limited the use of pyrotechnics. Now with the influx of additional troops, it is imperative that you immediately discontinue the use of those materials that would cause a wildfire.

Sincerely,
Gary Boushelle
Acting Deputy Director[31]

---

fire prevention and control measures, to include annual fire prevention meetings, mutual aid agreements, and actions to be taken in case of fire," listed Koppa.

Fire control measures were put into place over successive years of interdepartmental coordination. These measures have again been reviewed at the local level, and were found to be sufficient. As an example, pyrotechnic training devices were banned by Camp Grayling in late May, weeks before the fire.

Lt. Col. Koppa further explained methods that have improved in the last few years:

- Improvement of cleared fire breaks—Over fifteen miles of firebreak have been build and maintained, around the fenced artillery area.

Dan L. Alstott, AuSable Manistee Action Council

Night firing at Range 40 at Camp Grayling, the site of many fires in the past. This has recently been made a bit more fireproof. The military now pre-burns the entire 7,000 acre range impact area every year before their training season.

Chapter 7
Has the National Guard Been a Contributing Factor in Fire Situations Near Grayling?

- Allocation of firefighting equipment and resources—Camp Grayling has a full-time fire department during the summer training months. The department was expanded to four crews during the June encampment period.

- Prescribed burning—The practice of annually pre-burning those areas likely to catch fire later in the season, namely the artillery range impact area. This eliminates the fuel source and fire risk during peak danger times.

Both departments have reviewed the circumstances of the June 1992 fires. Their findings were that the fires did not endanger homes or personal property while confined to the range. They were found to be well within the control measures in place through previous coordination between the two departments. Therefore, allegations that the fires were out of control were unfounded. A continuing effort will be conducted to remedy the problem of smoke drifting over residential neighborhoods.

"By monitoring a fire, as opposed to extinguishing the fire," emphasized Camp Grayling's Fire Chief, CPT Steve Green, "the fire performs a useful purpose, clearing last year's dry grass and brush, so it will not be a hazard later in the training year. Within the impact area and fire break, a controlled burn poses no real threat to those outside the area. However, we will work on measures to limit smoke in the future."[32]

And that was about the way things went during the dry spell of 1992...it appeared as though short tempers were adequately defused. However, as the following newsprint articles demonstrate, this has been a continuing issue in the area.

☒ ☒ ☒ ☒ ☒

National Guard Fires–Part Two

Problems with fires reportedly originating through National Guard practices have resurfaced throughout the '80s and '90s. In 1988, several reports of guard fire problems were brought to light through news accountings.

☒   ☒   ☒   ☒   ☒

The AMAC (AuSable Manistee Action Council) published an impressive pamphlet, *Right in the Heart of Northern Michigan.* The front cover shows a group of "Danger" and "Warning" signs erupting from a "heart" located just to the west of I-75 where Grayling is located. The inside displays a full page colored map of Camp Grayling and the surrounding lands it uses for various types of military training. Some of the brochure's highlighted areas claim:

> **The upper AuSable and Manistee River Basins are natural resource treasures but they are currently occupied by the military.**

> **Camp Grayling's existing military training facility and planned future have a profound effect on the area.**

> **AMAC's current mission is to control the National Guard Expansion and misuse of the Camp Grayling Army and Air National Guard Training Site in Michigan.**

Chapter 7
Has the National Guard Been a Contributing Factor in Fire Situations Near Grayling?

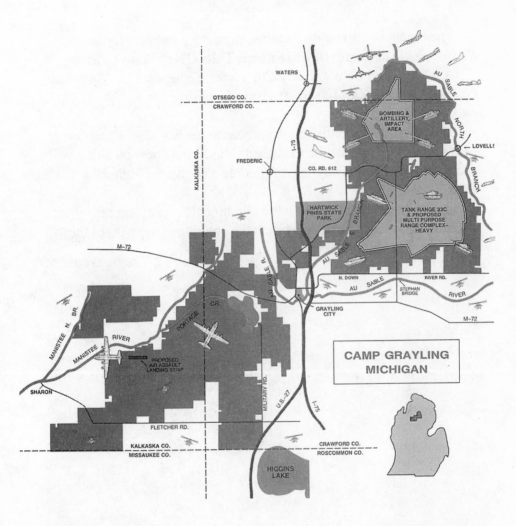

Ausable Manistee Action Council

Map of Camp Grayling in the AMAC's literature

The brochure also held a headline from the *Traverse City Record-Eagle* that read: **Defense Firms Take Over Camp Grayling.**

Another lifted from *The Bay City Times*, September 13, 1989 read: **Group Wants to Zap Lasers at Camp Grayling**[34]

The controversy continues, the problems persist. Most likely during each dry season that hits the Crawford County area, new incidents will occur between Camp Grayling, the people who live there, and the Michigan DNR.

On one hand it remains a matter of national security, on the other, vacationers and local residents resent the ongoing maneuvers of the troops. Only time will tell.

Coverage of the Mack Lake Fire 1980

At least two major, modern-day forest fires have been labeled controversial; one was the Seney Fire, the other was the Mack Lake Fire.

Why single out just these two? Both dealt in part with a prescription for fire gone wrong. Sadly, the Mack Lake blaze took the life of a departmental firefighter.

Mack Lake
Averages a Major Fire Once Every Twenty Years

MACK LAKE FIRE: July 1980. Burned 25,000 acres of the northern lower peninsula and destroyed 44 homes with 1,500 people evacuated; $2 million in damages and one U.S. Forest Service firefighter died in the blaze.

Donald Johnson, Fire Prevention Specialist, Department of Natural Resources–Forest Management Division, stated in an article, "FIRE" published in the March/April 1991 issue of *MICHIGAN Natural Resources* magazine:

More recently, the 1980 Mack Lake fire in Oscoda County destroyed 44 homes and buildings and took the life of a firefighter. There is evidence that several other large fires have occurred in the same area since 1920. The Perry Holt Fire destroyed five homes in Ogemaw County in 1988. The Stephan Bridge Road and Billman Road Fires in Crawford County in 1990 burned 86 homes, with property losses pegged at $5 million. Lest anyone think that only large fires in pine plantations are dangerous, on Halloween Day 1990 a person burning leaves in Cass County lost control of that fire. In a very short time, four homes were lost and a fifth one damaged.

Johnson also commented; "A raging wildfire may be controlled, contained or starved, but it is difficult to extinguish."[35]

Louis Borie wrote "Tragedy of the Mack Lake Fire," which appeared in the July 1981 issue of *American Forests* magazine. He too commented on the Mack Area being the epicenter of fire activity:

In the Mack Lake area, major fires have occurred every 20 years on the average, according to tree-ring data. A fire history in the area was compiled just after the Mack Lake fire. It showed that some trees had been scarred by a 16,000 acre fire that covered much of the same area in 1946, and some showed scarring from a major fire that occurred in 1913.[36]

A booklet entitled "The Mack Lake Fire" was published January 19, 1983 by the North Central Forest Experiment Station, Forest Service–U.S. Department of Agriculture, St. Paul, Minnesota, written by Albert J. Simard, Donald A. Haines, Richard W. Blank, and John S. Frost. With permission to reprint their drawn conclusions, their accounting follows:

1: The Mack Lake Fire was not unique. Five other fires in excess of 10,000 acres have occurred in the Mack Lake area since 1820. The average interval between major jack pine crown fires is 28 years. Large crown fires will continue to be an intermittent fact of life in jack pine forests.

2: In northern Lower Michigan, the spring fire season appears to be typified by wide fluctuations in fire danger. Ninety percent of the days are either too low or high, with less than 10 percent in between. Periods of moderate fire weather appropriate for prescribed burning rarely last more than one day. This complicates the prescribed burning planning process.

3: The Mack Lake Fire occurred just six days after ½ inch of rain fell. Only a slight precipitation deficit was recorded during the four months preceding the fire. It is clear that drought is not necessary for a major spring crown fire in jack pine. During the last four days of the drying period, relative humidity at 1300 ranged from 19 to 28 percent.

4: Horizontal roll vortices may be a common mechanism of lateral crown fire spread. If they form, they are a safety hazard for crews working on the flanks of crown fires. Further research into this phenomenon will be needed before the processes involved are understood and procedures for predicting the occurrence of horizontal roll vortices can be developed.

5: There are many large, relatively flat areas where jack pine predominates. Once a crown fire begins to run in this timber type, large-scale fire suppression efforts are needed. Fuel breaks, composed of less flammable hardwood species or widely spaced trees, could yield important fire suppression benefits such as reducing rate of spread and intensity, increasing firefighter safety, and providing an opportunity to make a stand.

6: The moisture content of old jack pine foliage is at a minimum during the onset of new growth in the spring. This increases crowning potential and may result in crown fire spread rates twice those encountered in the fall. These changes should be incorporated into fire management planning.

7: Several conditions contributed to the escape of the prescribed fire:

Spotting from slash piles.

Irregular groups of uncut trees adjacent to the prescribed fire area.

Locating the control line near the top of a 25-percent slope.

High windspeed (15-plus mph).

Low relative humidity (21 percent).

Low fire-fuel moisture (7 percent).

8: The transition from prescribed burning to wildfire control is critical. Subsequent spot fires can threaten initial attack crews. Since confusion is possible when an escape is attacked, it is important that the transition be planned in advance.

9: In jack pine, a fire can develop from an initial spot to a running crown fire in as little as 10 minutes and to project size in 20 minutes. This requires a rapid change in perspective by fire management personnel at all levels. Firefighters may have to shift from building line to escaping; dispatchers from moving crews to ordering overhead teams and fire camps; and the fire boss from control to community evacuation. Every member of an organization must immediately recognize the changed situation and take appropriate action.

10: The average rate of spread of the Mack Lake Fire (2 mph) was similar to that of other fast-moving crown fires. The maximum rate of spread (6 to 8 mph) equals the fastest recorded rate for which we had data.

11: During the fire's major run, average fireline intensity (8,800 BTU/ft/sec) was similar to that for other major crown fires. The 1-hour maximum fireline intensity (15,500 BTU/ft/sec) was less than that for three major fires for which we had data. The 15-minute peak intensity (29,500 BTU/ft/sec) may have approximated an upper limit for moving crown fires.

12: The number of permanent and seasonal residences in and adjacent to wild land areas is increasing. Noting that two out of three homes in Mack Lake did not burn, an expanded program should be developed to explain to homeowners the potential for wildfire damage and how to locate and landscape their homes to prevent loss.[37]

Donald Haines

Fire front of the Mack Lake Fire

Why was it so important to prescribe a controlled burn during such a period of drought? This was prime Kirtland's Warbler habitat and the forest service is dedicated to preserving its rare form of habitat. At least today we've learned that jack pine country of the Lower Peninsula is not the only nesting site for this seemingly endangered species.

Richard P. Smith in his "Regional Report" column for **Michigan Out-of-Doors,** October 1998 issue, stated, "Fourteen singing male Kirtland's warblers were counted in the Upper Peninsula during June. Six were seen in Schoolcraft County, five in Marquette County, and three in Delta County. Females were observed with males in each county, confirming the potential of continued reproduction in the region. A lone male also was spotted in northern Wisconsin."[38]

With Kirtland's warblers expanding their nesting/breeding territories into new and varied terrains, perhaps future prescriptions for fire will be more carefully tended in jack pine country.

Following the Mack Lake disaster, a burned out homeowner, Joe Walker, commented, "I hope that warbler enjoys his nest...my nest is burned."

The above mentioned controlled burn was regarded as being, "The Crane Lake Unit prescribed burn." It is one of several such areas under the management of the U.S. Forest Service and the Michigan DNR for Kirtland's warbler habitat control acting under the federal Endangered Species Act. Their combined goal was to create approximately 3,000 acres of habitat each year until 1990.[39]

The Crane Lake burn had been cancelled twice previously, which is not uncommon due to a scarcity of suitable burning days in this specific area.

The Crane Lake/Mack Lake burn should be held up as an example; a prescribed 210 acre section of Kirtland's warbler habitat quickly grew out of proportion, reaching over 25,000 total acres before the fire ran its course. One life was lost. Even one life is too many to save an endangered species.

At the start of this chapter we mentioned that other fires plagued the Mack Lake area both before and after this large fire. The Library of *The Detroit Free Press* provided the following feature story:

Detroit Free Press, July 3, 1988
Byline: Tom Opre

Drought Conditions Worry Michigan's Forest Fire Staff

LANSING—An understaffed, underfunded brigade of state forest firefighters is all that nervously faces an already extreme and rapidly growing threat of millions in wildfire losses and damage stemming from this summer's drought conditions.

Forest fire staff administrators in the Department of Natural Resources are quick to praise their agency's modern tactics as "the best in the nation." They brag about doing more with less than anyone else. But even they admit that the tinder dry conditions, too few trained people and, in some cases, aging equipment may be a scenario for disaster.

So far, every fire outbreak has been contained. DNR fire crews have been on full alert for months, however, and overtime budgets "went into the end a long time ago," said Don Grant, assistant Chief of the DNR's Forest Management Division and the men charged with protecting millions of acres of state forests.

His assessment? "We are in grave danger right now of a major fire...a truly costly one," Grant said.

"Heaven forbid that more than one large fire should break out at once. Our resources are already stretched to the limit."

Scott Heather, assistant forester for the DNR's northern Lower Peninsula region, said his fire officers were working 70 to 80 hour weeks.

"When you have fires burning, you can't just tell a guy to go home because the money has run out," he said.

Extremely dry conditions prompt two problems: One, more fires break out. Forty fires weekly is normal in the northern Lower Peninsula…a five-year average of 352 fires annually. This year, DNR crews…often assisted by local fire departments and U.S. Forest Service experts…already have fought 438 fires. And July and August are traditionally "hot" months. Two, up to 400 percent more time is needed to suppress each fire. Prolonged dryness leeches all moisture from organic debris covering the soil.

Fires not only burn over the top of the ground, they burn down into it, smoldering down a foot or more.

"That takes time to root out and snuff," Heather said. "A two-acre fire near Roscommon last week should have taken an hour to suppress. But fire officers worked eight hours…until midnight…and still had to go back the next morning to douse smoldering hot spots."

The ultra-dryness is "truly scary," Heather said. Needle moisture readings in jack pine, a measure of combustibility, were "the lowest I've seen this May," he said, and after a brief return in early June, are headed down once again.

The only thing between

Donald Haines

Mack Lake, May 5, 1980—a column of smoke billows high into the air

the woods and disaster, Heather said, was the wind. "Give us a big outbreak on a really windy day and look out," he said. When asked about stopping a big fire lacking manpower and machines, another field officer quipped, "Well, there's always Lake Huron." It was a reference to huge fires that repeatedly burned over much of the Upper and northern Lower Peninsula following the lumber era at the turn of the century.

Whole towns disappeared when fires raced dozens of miles. People were killed. Such fires either died out in rainstorms or burned their way to the lakeshore.

Michigan's firefighting system is mechanized wherever possible, unique in the nation. A one-man tractor plows a fire break, churning the earth bare. That is followed by a two-man 4x4 pumper unit that douses flames jumping the fire line and protects the tractor operator...so valuable in front of the approaching fire.

"These must be trained people, knowledgeable in fire behavior," Heather said.

Michigan has about 115 pumpers of various capacities, Grant said, and more than 100 tractors. But there is not enough personnel to man them...or to keep them repaired. Thanks to low state budgets in the late 1970s and early 1980s, retiring specialists were not replaced.

Grant estimates that more than half the tanker and tractor fleet is more than a decade old. "Quite a few" he could provide no accurate count are more than 20 years old.

Newly appointed DNR director David Hales agreed that his agency's firefighting capacity was "in dire straits." "Last week at one fire alone three machines broke down," Hales said, "and had to be repaired on the line." Mechanics are "making heroic efforts and doing magic stuff to keep all those machines going," he said, "but we must provide help. We don't just throw people at fires, we throw technical expertise and equipment."

More large bulldozers are needed, Hales said, and the heavy trailers to transport them. Unfortunately, all the needs are big-ticket items...very costly machines. He pointed out that eight new fire officer positions...all the division had requested...were approved recently. Twenty-two temporary workers were hired, too.

Yet Grant said that "40 to 45 more" fire officers were needed to bring the crews to full staffing. Only 142 people are in fire control today, compared to 247 in 1978. A staff of 180 to 185, thanks to the mechanized approach, "could keep us current with the addition of some new equipment," Grant said.

Grant said the division would also like to rebuild the forest fire experiment station near Roscommon. Every piece of firefighting machinery bought is rebuilt there to department specifications. The current station opened in 1929 and is still the only such state-run facility in the nation.

"If more than one large fire were to break out simultaneously, the thin line of protection might snap," Heather said.

"The prospect really frightens me," he said, "because then we may be forced to chose between buildings and forest. If we dedicate the available force to saving buildings, maybe the fire grows quickly out of control and we end up losing much more than we saved elsewhere."

Donald Haines

The Mack Lake Fire jumps a roadway

Crown fires…those burning up into the tops of dry trees…can cover ground at great speed in high winds.

"I lived in terror last weekend when it was bone dry with 30–40-knot winds," Hales said. "Lots of people were out in the woods…just as they will be this weekend."

Among the things most likely to spark a big fire outbreak are power lines downed by high winds and careless burning of debris or untended campfires. Cigarettes tossed from car windows start many fires too.

Gov. James Blanchard has banned all outside burning as the drought continues.[40] *(Reprinted by permission of the Detroit Free Press)*

Case Study: Mack Lake Fire

Note: This case study was prepared by the National Fire Protection Association, Quincy, MA, and sponsored by the National Wildland Urban Interface Fire Protection Initiative.

Mack Lake Fire

The Mack Lake Fire is worthy of note because it occurred in similar terrain and jack pine fuels in the next county east of Crawford County. (In retrospect to the Stephan Bridge Road Fire). It destroyed 44 homes and buildings, burned 25,000 acres starting on May 5, 1980. One firefighter died in the fire. The incident began as a prescribed fire, but it spotted across a highway and became a wildfire. In the first 3 hours the fire advanced 7 miles. No amount of fire line or road width held or slowed the fire. Changing fuels and weather conditions later slowed the fire and allowed the fire crews to build 35 miles of fire line to contain the fire 30 hours after it started.

In consuming 270,000 tons of fuel the fire released 3,000,000,000 BTU of energy, or nine times the energy released by the Hiroshima atomic bomb. Investigator/researchers determined that within the area burned by the Mack Lake fire, there have probably been five other fires in excess of 10,000 acres since 1820, for an average of one major fire every 28 years.

A report on the fire by the USDA Forest Service contained this discussion about local weather conditions:

The most severe fire weather in Michigan normally occurs when the Lake States are on the northwest or back edge of a...high pressure area. Generally, air masses and associated frontal systems move through the region in a southeasterly direction every 3 to 5 days. When a high pressure system persists longer than normal, however, fuels have more time to dry out. The approach of a cold front aggravates the situation by increasing the flow of dry, warm air from the southwest. Consequently, peak fire danger is expected when the Lake States have been under extended high pressure influence just before the passage of a cold front, as happened, for example, prior to the Peshtigo and Great Chicago fires of 1871 (Haines and Kuehnast 1970). Precipitation associated with frontal passage normally ends the period of high fire danger."

Almost all of the conditions of the Mack Lake fire were present at the Stephan Bridge Road fire, reminding us of the powerful effect of fire weather and certain fuels.

Weather conditions: The Mack Lake fire area suffered from hot (the high was 17 degrees higher than the average maximum for May) and dry (21 percent at the lowest point, compared to a May average of 51 percent) weather immediately before the blaze. A cold front moved through and at 2:00 P.M. produced a wind speed of 15–18 mph with gusts of 25–30 mph.

Topography: The fire was on a plateau with very little variation of elevation. The area is very similar to the topography of Crawford County.

Fuel types and arrangement: The predominate fuel was jack pine growing on sandy soil which dries rapidly after a rain. Other timber types and understory vegetation were similar to that in the Stephan Bridge Road fire. On average, 19 tons of jack pine fuel per acre were present before the fire. About 6,000 of the acres burned had pre-fire. About 6,000 of the acres burned had predominantly hardwood stands on better soils. Fuel loading in a typical sedge area was 3.5 tons per acre, also similar to the Stephan Bridge Road fire.

Fire spread and intensity: During its major run the fire spread at an average rate of 2.1 mph, similar to the Stephan Bridge Road fire. At that time the average fireline intensity was calculated at 8,800 BTU/ft/sec.

The limit of manual control is established as 100 BTU/ft/sec; the limit where spotting would be expected to present serious control problems for mechanical equipment. The fire continued to spread until the relative humidity increased to 55 percent and the fire burned into hardwood stands that burned slower than the jack pine.

Fire spotting: The prescribed fire escaped control because of spotting. It was later observed spotting at least ¼ mile ahead of the front. A research model by Albini predicts spot fire distances from burning trees. A 5-inch thick, 25-foot high jack pine in a 15-mph wind indicates a one-third mile maximum spotting distance during a major run. Higher winds extend the spotting distance.[41]

Chronology: Mack Lake Fire

Note: The chronology of the Mack Lake Fire appears through the courtesy of the North Central Forest Experiment Station, Forest Service–U. S. Department of Agriculture, St. Paul, Minnesota.

Between 1022 and 1026 (May 5)

The Crane Lake prescribed burn was ignited. No unusual fire activity was noted for the first 45 minutes. Piled slash burned vigorously, with flame lengths of 10–15 feet, but flame lengths between the piles were only 6–12 inches. Although some spot fires crossed the control line, they were easily contained and firing resumed. During the next 45 minutes, three more spot fires occurred, one required a double plow line to contain.

At 1206

The prescribed fire spotted into standing jack pine timber adjacent to and upslope of the prescribed fire area. Being on the windward edge of a hill, the stand was exposed to the wind; this, coupled with heavier fuel loading, including bracken fern, resulted in a much faster spread rate than had been experienced in the prescribed burn area. The fire spread eastward toward Highway 33,675 feet away, with scorch heights ranging from 1–6 feet. A tractor-plow attempted to contain the spot between the prescribed burn and the highway.

Between 1215 and 1230

The fire spotted across Highway 33. This may have resulted from the burning slash piles or from the spot fire torching a small group of trees at the edge of the highway. The first spot across the highway had scorch heights of 2–4 feet and was contained at three-fourths of an acre. A second spot (225 feet from the fire), first noted at 15 feet in diameter, was attacked by a tractor-plow within 4 minutes of detection. At this time, considerable smoke was reported across Highway 33, hampering visibility. The spot torched some trees within 25 feet of the point of origin and then dropped to the ground in a narrow strip of mature jack pine. The fire boss recalled a sudden increase in windspeed at this time. The fire entered an extensive sapling-sized jack pine stand and crowned within 100 feet of the point of origin. Surface fuel at the point of crowning was primarily sedge combined with pine litter and duff.

Between 1232 and 1245

The fire front was ½ mile east of Highway 33, and spotting at least ¼ mile ahead. The tractor-plow was now working the north flank. An armored tanker started following and eventually passed the tractor-plow. The tractor-plow operator was trapped shortly after being passed by the tanker. The tanker crew reported that they never saw the head of the fire, despite traveling at 4–6 mph while spraying water. Although the fire was on the ground close to where the crew was working (flame heights of 1–2 feet), torching and crowning were visible 100–200 feet inside the line (flame heights of 30–40 feet). The fire was described by the crew as turbulent with "heavy, roiling black smoke." The wind shifted direction several times and the fire frequently fingered in a northerly direction. The fire was reported to be "…very sensitive to wind. A slight change in wind direction and a hot flank immediately turned into a crowning head." The changes were described as instantaneous. In the words of the tanker operator, "I'm sure that the main head of the fire was heading east, but the flanks were acting like the head of many fires I've been on."

…The evidence of a northward moving crown fire approximately 100 feet east of the point where the tractor abruptly turned northward is consistent with a local north wind resulting from the downdraft portion of a vortex. There is also evidence of an eastward moving crown fire (originating from spots which crossed the line behind the tractor) approximately 200 feet north of the tractor's final position. Once established, the latter crown fire was presumably beyond the influence of the vortex and responded to ambient winds. The tractor-plow and operator were trapped between the two fires while the tanker (approximately 100 yards ahead) was able to turn northward and escape.

Because other scenarios could be reasonably consistent with the physical evidence, we cannot prove that our hypothesis is what actually transpired. However, all other possibilities we considered do not appear to agree with the physical evidence as well as that postulated here. Therefore, although we have described what, in our opinion, is the most likely sequence of events, further research on the formation of horizontal roll vortices will be needed to confirm or refute our hypothesis.

At 1310

The fire crossed County Road 489. It was approaching the village of Mack Lake, which had been evacuated. Photographs indicated flame heights of twice the height of the trees (20–30 feet). The fire boss reported that "a wall of fire" was approaching the village. He was "impressed with its consistency." He reported flame heights 20–30 feet above the trees. These observations suggest flame heights ranging from 40–60 feet. The fire was still spotting at least mile ahead.

At 1325

The fire had passed through the village of Mack Lake. Forty-four homes and cottages (about one out of three) were destroyed. Although a study was not conducted, a general impression is that homes with mowed lawns and some distance between them and the jack pine forest survived. Those in minimal clearings with natural vegetation and/or with firewood piled adjacent to the house did not.

By this time, the fire was ½ mile east of Forest Service Road 4146. At about this time, a second report indicated that the fire had spread along County Road 604 from Forest Service Road 4458 to 4460 (2 miles) in 15

Donald Haines

Aerial view of Mack Lake fire area taken three weeks after the fire

minutes. These observations indicate spread rates of 6–8 mph—the fastest reported spread rates during the fire's run. One observer remarked that it was "notably warmer" when the fire was still ½ mile away. The flames were described as similar to movies of the sun, with isolated balls of flame in the air. Another observer noted that, "Following the crown fire, un-burned ground fuels ignited and burned in all directions This could imply that during the major run, the crown fire was independent of the ground fire. This observation could also describe a crown fire which gained momentum from spot fires and raced ahead of the surface fire for some distance before dropping back to the ground. Surface fuels ignite from material that drops from the burning overstory. Such "semi-independent" crown fire behavior was reported on the Gaston Fire in South Carolina. It is in the areas burned during this period that the largest unbroken areas of crown fire are found.

At 1530

The fire was at the junction of County Road 489 and Forest Service Road 4461. The wind had shifted to west-northwest and the fire was now spreading east-southeast on a wide front. Although the fire was still spreading rapidly, the rate of advance had slowed slightly.

At 1600

The fire was ½ mile east of Forest Service Road 4527 along County Road 604. This sector of the fire had passed from jack pine to hardwoods and was burning on the ground. The northeast corner of the fire had become a flank, and control actions were becoming effective. Most of the front, however, was still actively crowning in jack pine.

At 1825

The fire was reported to be 4–5 miles northwest of South Branch. Since the final perimeter was 5 miles northwest the fire was perhaps 5½ miles away at the time. This is 1½ miles from the 1600 position. The wind

Donald Haines

Mack Lake Fire...a town in peril

had shifted to north-northeast. What had been the southern flank was not the fire front. Although most of the fuel burned during this period was jack pine, the crown fire appears to have weakened. A random sample of an aerial photomosaid indicates that in the area burned during this period, an average of 30 percent of the crown foliage was not consumed. Since both wind and fuels remained constant, we presume that this change largely reflected increased relative humidity which by 1800, had risen to 55 percent. During this period, video tapes of the fire taken along Highway 33 show backfire flame heights of 12–18 inches in jack pine surface fuels. Flame heights in 2–2-foot-deep fresh slash were 5–10 feet, however. Thus, although the fire had slowed, it still presented control problems, particularly where fuel loadings were high. High crown scorch heights of isolated red and jack pine trees in the hardwood areas attest to the fact that even though the fire burned on the ground, it was still moderately intense.

By 2400

The fire spread an additional ½ mile to the east and south, primarily on the ground, through hardwood stands. Mechanized equipment could now work effectively on all sections of the perimeter.

By 0600 (May 6)

The fire had essentially stopped spreading. Suppression forces had constructed 15 miles of control line.

By 1800

The fire was contained at 23,830 acres, with 35 miles of control line. There was no significant increase in acreage burned during the day. Little difficulty was experienced in burning out from plowed control lines.

It is important to note that during the four days following passage of the same dry cold front that affected the Mack Lake Fire, a forest fire in Alberta increased from 20,000 to 150,000 acres in size. Therefore, it is reasonable to assume that if the Mack Lake Fire had not run out of jack pine, the total area burned would have been significantly larger.[42]

Horizontal Roll Vertices and Crown Fires

By Donald A. Haines

Note: The rest of this paper is reprinted in Chapter Four, The Fletcher Road Fire.

3. Case Histories
a. The Mack Lake Fire

Air reconnaissance of this Michigan crown fire showed long streets of unburned (although often scorched) conifer crowns in an otherwise vast area of blackened ground and trees. (Simard et al., 1982). These tree-crown streets crossed roads and gently rolling terrain but still essentially maintained their identity, often for 3–6 km and in one case for more than 11 km. Crown streets were most often parallel to each other, although clusters of parallel streets diverged (usually near the fire's origin) or converged (usually near the fire's termination). Individual streets were reasonably straight; a few curved toward the major fire activity. Distance between parallel streets ranged from 45 to 850 m. Width of individual streets ranged from less than 10 to 200 m. From the air, some sides of streets appeared ragged; others were smooth, suggesting strong fire activity along them.

Tree-trunk char and scorch resulting from wildland fires is highest on the downwind side. Ground examination of the crown-street understory at Mack Lake invariably disclosed that the low-charred sides of tree trunks faced each other. This phenomenon indicated that fire had speed in opposite directions from winds radiating outward from within all streets. The car height was generally 0.3–1 m on the insides of the tree trunks and 1.5–3 m on the opposite sides. The center line of opposing spread tended to be offset toward the side where the fire had been most active when streets were formed. Center lines were generally located from one-fourth to one-third the width of the street from the strong fire side. On wide streets there was often no charring along the center line; even needles suspended a few centimeters from the ground were not burned or scorched. Some trees with char or scorch on opposing sides were less than 1 m apart, but most were 1.5–3 m apart. Char was most prominent in the direction of forward fire spread when trees with opposing patterns were less than 1.5 m apart. These understory patterns continued along all streets examined.

When the crown street and understory pattern became disorganized, it invariably re-formed within a short distance. Investigation showed that it had changed for one of the following reasons:

1) A single, uncharred tree street had re-formed into two or more streets, or multiple streets had reformed into single streets. This was always accompanied by a change in the overhead tree-crown pattern.

2) The street was 60–90 m upwind of an intersecting road. The street and understory pattern usually re-formed 15–25 m on the other side of the road.

In one instance the uncharted street moved from conifers to hardwoods. Even though there was no crowning in the latter, the uncharted street continued along a sidehill 60 m high with a 25° slope, 45 m up from the bottom. The pattern indicated that along the length of this hill the fire had burned downslope below the street and upslope above the street.

A portion of the Mack Lake fire was videotaped from the air during the fire's major burning period. The tape shows strong buoyancy on the forward sector of the fire's north flank, as evidenced by heavy smoke rising more than 2 km into the atmosphere. However, toward the trailing sector of the same flank, there appears to be a HRV. A comparison with ground features indicates that this smoke-outlined eddy is more than 3 km long and 0.4 km in diameter. The structure seems to be distinct and uniform. Videotape taken -3 h later shows another possible HRV, this one located along the southern flank. Because of poor viewing angle and no ground reference, its diameter or length could not be estimated. Simard et al. (1982) give additional information including a synoptic mesoscale analysis of this fire.

A Table showed background information on crown fires. Mack Lake was included:

Mack Lake:	Huron National Forest, Michigan	May 5, 1980	10040 acres burned	Videotape of two vortices	Sapling to small pole jack pine	Temp=28°C RH=21-26% Wind=16-29 48 km h

Comments: Initial 7300 hm burned in 6 hours. Flame height = 10–25 m[43]

Escanaba's "Stockyard Fire"
July, 1988

The most volatile tree growing in the forest is the jack pine...learn why fires of this type crown...learn of hazards firefighters may incur...learn about air tanker vortex turbulence.

Escanaba's "Stockyard Fire"—July 1988

Actually, it was not really a "stockyard fire." The site previously had been a stockyard, but the district during modern times was well-wooded with pines and deemed rural land. So in essence, the "Stockyard Fire" was in reality a wildfire. Feature stories describing the blaze appeared in *The Detroit Free Press*.

Detroit Free Press, July 2, 1988
David Jones, Free Press Staff Writer

Forest Blaze Injures Two in U.P.

Fire raced through 1,700 acres of the drought-dry Hiawatha National Forest in the Upper Peninsula near Escanaba Friday night, forcing the evacuation of 60 families, injuring two firefighters and temporarily closing U.S.-2 to holiday weekend traffic.

More than 80 firefighters from 12 communities, the U.S. Forest Service and the state Department of Natural Resources struggled to contain the blaze, which officials said began north of the highway but was driven by wind two miles south into the Stonington Peninsula.

"If it was not so dry the fire would not have moved so fast and it would not be so intense," said Mary Mumford, spokeswoman for the national forest.

The two-month-old drought has left much of Michigan's woodlands perilously dry, and officials were aware of increased fire danger with the influx of campers and tourists for the summer holiday.

No cause of the fire was immediately determined.

Air tankers and helicopters made water drops every 15 minutes, but officials said the fire would likely burn through the night. The highway, a main artery into the camping and tourist areas of the U.P., reopened about 8:30 P.M. after being closed for 3½ hours, state police said.

A DNR firefighter was to be flown to Milwaukee for treatment of burns at St. Mary's Hospital, Mumford said. The other was treated for smoke inhalation and released from St. Francis Hospital in Escanaba, about 14 miles west of the fire scene across Little Bay De Noc.

Mumford said Rapid River High School was turned into an evacuation center.

Two buildings were badly damaged, but six homes were saved by firefighters who diverted the blaze.

Donald Haines

Tons of smoke billow upward from the Stockyard Fire

The disruption on U.S.-2 was the only highway problem reported in Michigan as the Fourth of July holiday period began.[44] *(Reprinted by permission of the Detroit Free Press)*

Newspaper accountings present the bare bones facts of any story. Usually, there is far more to report on than meets the eye. Questions went unanswered. How was the firefighter so severely burned? What happened?

Answers came from Don Haines, former Principal Research Meteorologist for East Lansing's Fire Project, who had retired to Stuart, Florida in 1989. Haines provided excellent slides taken at the Stockyard Fire and included an article he had written on vortex turbulence for ***Fire Manage-***

ment Notes. In the article, Don describes a crown fire that suddenly erupted into "a breaking wave," in other words, a horizontal roll vortex. Most interesting was his subsequent finding that a DC-4 air tanker carrying two thousand gallons of retardant had flown along the fire line, circled, and came back to drop the retardant just south of the sector as the fire intensified. An invisible sheet of turbulent air left in the wake of the aircraft caused the fire to "climb" and become a high wall of flames, destroying a tractor and seriously injuring the driver.

Air Tanker Vortex Turbulence... Revisited

Donald A. Haines
Research Meteorologist, USDA Forest Service,
North Central Forest Experiment Station, East Lansing, MI

The Stockyard Fire

Extreme drought had a devastating impact on wildland fire activity over much of the Central and Western United States during the summer and autumn of 1988. State and Federal suppression forces in Michigan's Upper Peninsula confronted fire behavior rarely experienced in early summer, typically a period of low fire occurrence.

The Stockyard Fire, near Escanaba, MI, proved especially troublesome because of unexpected fire behavior. Among other features, 100-foot-long (30-m) sheets of flame moved horizontally, undulating like waves on a water surface. Fire brands moving with the sheets caused spot fires that quickly turned into 15- to 30-foot-high (4.5- to 9-m) fire whirlwinds. Even though the Burning Index (National Fire Danger Rating System) was 27 with fuel model E, burning was so intense along some sectors of the fire that escaping gases did not ignite until well above the fire. In those cases, the gases exploded as large bubbles high in the air.

But the most interesting behavior occurred along a 300-foot (91 m) length of the right flank. Here three tractor-plow operators built line within a jack pine plantation. The trees were 3 to 6 inches (8 to 15 cm) in diameter and 25 to 30 feet (715 to 9 m) high. Compared with other sectors, this was a quiet area. The operators plowed 50 feet (15 m) from a backing fire with 2-foot (0.6-m) flame lengths. Aided by a firing-out crew well behind

Donald Haines

The aftermath—charred pine tree corpses

the tractor operators, the fire burned to the line, leaving a wide black area.

Winds were light and then became calm. The low flames suddenly began to "climb" up a few trees into the crowns. Within a minute or two, the flames became a high wall. The wall changed into a crown fire, moving directly toward the tractor crew. Flame tilt had shifted from slightly eastward to vertical and then to westward.

The resultant crown fire was described as a "waterfall," a "breaking wave," a "curl," and a "wave curl." In other words, it was a horizontal roll vortex of some type. Witnesses also stated that this wave (vortex) moved along the fire line at about 15 miles per hour (24 km/h). The vortex rotation threw foot-long (0.3-m) firebrands westward, 100 feet (30 m) away from the flank, into unburned fuels. Flame heights increased to 150 to 250 feet (45 to 76 m). Luckily no one was killed, although one of the tractor operators was badly injured and spent weeks in a medical burn center.

What happened? Of equal interest, why did it happen only along this one section of the line?

Possibilities Rejected

None of the more typical causes can explain the unexpected changes in fire behavior. There were no heavy fuel concentrations. Fuels were relatively uniform in a typical jack pine plantation. Also, the area was relatively flat with no unusual topographic features.

There were no apparent immediate weather concerns. The weather charts showed that the region was covered by a large, flat, high-pressure cell. Although the fire occurred near one of the Great Lakes, the land/sea breeze circulation did not change at that time. Also there was no apparent change in the vertical structure of the atmosphere over the fire.

Burnout operations upstream of the site had no effect on downstream activity nor did anyone see the formation of a large vertical fire whirl or other suspicious fire-initiated features.

Lessons Relearned

However, one interesting incident did occur in this sector only minutes before the sudden, violent increase in fire activity. A DC-4 air tanker carrying 2,000 gallons (7,571 l) of retardant flew along the fire line, circled, then came back and dropped the retardant just south of this sector as the fire intensified. The tanker was flying as less than 400 feet (122 m) and at perhaps 140 miles per hour (225 km/h).

Almost a quarter of a century ago, Davis and Chandler published an article in *Fire Control Notes,* "Vortex turbulence...its effect on fire behavior." In it they warned about aircraft vortex turbulence, a sheet of turbulent air left in the wake of all aircraft. It rolls up into a strong vortex pair...two, compact, fast-spinning funnels of air. Unfortunately, this vortex pair is usually invisible.

Under certain conditions, the two vortices may stay close together, sometimes undulating slightly as they stretch rearward. The interaction between them tends to make them stay together as they move downward through the air. They usually roll apart as they hit the surface of the ground. This vortex phenomenon was discovered when it caused the crash of several light aircraft caught in the wakes of large airplanes.

Ordinarily, aircraft vortex turbulence does not endanger fire control forces. But, Davis and Chandler warned that under special circumstances, vortex wakes may cause fire behavior to change dramatically.

Vortex severity and persistence vary with several factors. Most important are the type, size, speed and altitude of the aircraft and the prevailing atmospheric conditions. Other factors being equal, the strongest vortex pair is produced by a large, slow-flying aircraft with a high wingspan loading. The speed is most important before landing or after takeoff. It is also a factor when an air tanker slows down for an accurate airdrop.

Aircraft altitude is important because vortices weaken rapidly with time. Under typical wind speeds, the vortex pair may lose its potential impact in less than a minute. But the pair tends to persist in calm air. At high altitude, the two vortices remain separated by a distance slightly less than the aircraft's wingspan. However, the interaction of the vortices causes them to drop at a rate of 300 to 500 feet per minute (515 to 9 km/in) depending on various factors.

Be Aware

Today's fire crews and air tanker pilots would be wise to heed the warnings offered by Davis and Chandler. Fire crews should be alert for trouble in these circumstances:

- The air is still and calm.

- The fire is burning in open land or in scattered or low timber.

- The air tanker is large or heavily loaded.

- The air tanker is flying low and slowly.

Air tanker pilots should be aware of the problem the aircraft can cause and take these precautions:

- Do not fly parallel to the fire line more than necessary.

- Keep high except when making the actual drop.

- Ensure that ground crews are alert to the presence of an air tanker and the intended flight path.[45]

Taking a Look at the DNR's Forest Fire Experiment Station Roscommon, Michigan

DNR's Forest Fire Experiment Station at Roscommon has designed and manufactured thousands of pieces of forest firefighting equipment for the State of Michigan that is not available commercially. Through federal and regional agreements, the staff also designs and tests equipment for forest fire agencies in twenty other northeastern states. The center's unique hydraulic plow used in firefighting has been described as the best in the world. Established in 1929 at a cost of about $50,000, the Station has saved the state millions of dollars in providing the equipment over the years.

Natural Resources Register—February 1987

Taking a Look at the DNR's
Forest Fire Experiment Station
Roscommon, Michigan

A Look Backward First

To better understand the future, we must first look at the past. The following description of early firefighting equipment was detailed in a 1950 booklet coauthored by J.A. Mitchell and D. Robson (Michigan Department of Conservation and U.S. Department of Agriculture) titled *Forest Fires and Forest Fire Control in Michigan: Equipment Development.*

While the principles of fire control remain the same there has been a vast change in equipment and techniques used in fighting forest fires since organized fire control got under way. The standard equipment of the pioneer fire warden was a round pointed shovel, a pail, and a pocket full of matches. Each firefighter furnished his own tools. Small fires were put out by scratching a line around them and covering burning logs and stumps with dirt or perhaps wetting them down with water from a nearby stream. Backfiring from roads or natural barriers was the usual procedure on large fires. The first state-owned equipment consisted of 18 longhandled shovels purchased to equip firefighters on a large fire about 1912. This purchase was questioned by the Auditor General and it was six months or more before the bill was paid. Furnishing tools for firefighters later became the rule, and a supply of shovels, axes, and saws has since been kept at each district headquarters for this purpose.

Horse-drawn plows, hired from local farmers, were used occasionally when available, but plows did not become standard equipment until the advent of the tractor. Very little use was made of water, although one old-time fire warden recalls carrying around a garden sprinkler to wet down grass fires ahead of the shovelmen. With the development of the back pack pump about 1920, the use of water became general and led eventually to the use of power pumps and tankers.

The State purchased its first tractor in 1917 for use in fire line construction on the Higgins Lake State Forest. Not until some years later, however, was power equipment provided for fire suppression. Its extensive use dates from Civilian Conservation Corps (CCC) days.

Transportation has always been a major problem. The early state fire wardens traveled on foot or by horse and buggy and were dependent on local help for fire suppression. Hand and foot operated railroad "speeders" or velocipedes were also used in patrolling railroad rights-of-way and reaching otherwise inaccessible areas.

Use of automobiles dates from about 1915. In its annual report for 1916, the Public Domain Commission points with pride to its "flying squadrons," two or more fire wardens with a Model T Ford, organized to take action on major fires. In 1917 automobiles were purchased for use on

photo courtesy Michigan DNR—Greg Lusk Collection

Hoses ran off car batteries in earlier firefighting methods

the State Forests. Fire wardens, however, continued to furnish their own transportation and haul firefighters on a mileage basis. In 1928 the Conservation Commission authorized the purchase of 12 trucks for fire control work, chiefly for the hauling of firefighters, supplies and tools.

About the same time, light trailers were provided for hauling supplies and equipment, and all forest officers' cars were fitted with trailer hitches.

Horse-drawn plows early demonstrated their usefulness for fire line construction but were handicapped by lack of power for tough going. The use of tractors overcame the power difficulty but made heavier and sturdier plows necessary.

Since 1930 the Department of Conservation has operated a Forest Fire Experiment Station at Roscommon that has specialized in fire equipment testing and development. This Station has contributed materially to the standardization and development of forest fire equipment and is largely responsible for the progress that has been made in Michigan in this direction. With a modern, fully equipped pattern and machine shop, and a full-time staff of mechanics and technicians, it has been in a position to design, test, modify, and build pilot models of promising fire control Equipment and to prepare specifications for their manufacture.[46]

Still continuing with the history, the DNR Forest Fire Experiment Station issued a brochure describing their past, present and future. Text taken from this publication follows:

Michigan's Forest Fire Experiment Station
What It Is: What It Does

History: The Forest Fire Experiment Station was founded in 1929 by the State of Michigan to develop methods of controlling the great wildfires that swept the Lake States following the indiscretions of the Lumbering Era. The United States Forest Service joined in this venture, housing their scientists on station grounds until the early 1950's.

The majority of the station's buildings were constructed by the Civilian Conservation Corps (CCC) in the early 1930's. The Station administers about 6,000 acres of land dedicated to fire research. It is located in the heart of Michigan's jack pine sand plains.

The first subjects studied were fire weather, fuels, fire behavior, fire damage, chemicals, and fire breaks. In subsequent years the emphasis shifted to firefighting methods and equipment development. In 1936 mechanics and machinists were employed for the manufacture of newly developed equipment. Commercial pumpers, crawler-tractors and trucks came more noticeably into use. By 1940, the art of fire control had progressed from the use of shovels and backpack pump cans to the utilization of powerful machinery.

Today, the Experiment Station has a staff of eleven, which includes engineers, mechanics, machinists, a draftsman, welder, forester and secretary. Computers have recently been acquired to assist with engineering design, drafting and business administration. In the 1980's our progress may not be measured so much by the appearance of what we produce as by the technology we apply to achieve our goals.

Development: The Forest Fire Experiment Station is known for its design of specialized forest fire equipment. The fireline plow development began in 1930, by modifying and strengthening horse drawn agricultural plows for rugged use in the woods. Late in that decade, the first double bottom sulky plows were designed and produced for fire use. By the 1950's, the hydraulic Michigan fireline plow had evolved, providing one of the most efficient fireline production tools available for eastern soils.

Wildfire pumper development has had an equally important role in the suppression of forest fires. The station began its first program of designing and testing off-the-road forest fire tankers following World War II. The station has since designed multi-axle drive tankers from 50 gallon to 1500 gallon capacity, using both commercial and military trucks.

Through the years many development problems have been tackled, including trenchers, large and small sandcasters, water pickup & drop systems for small aircraft, hydraulic water pumps, fire chemical application systems, specialized tankers made from crawler-tractors and skidders, well-jetting tools, and specialized spray nozzle systems. These development activities aim to produce more efficient fire suppression, with the goal of taking a concept from the drawing board to actual field use in the shortest possible time.

Research: As the name "Forest Fire Experiment Station" implies, the initial purpose of the organization was fire research. Fire behavior studies have recently been left to more specialized units of other agencies, but research continues on the use of fire chemicals, fire effects, forest fuel modification and fire break construction.

Recently concluded projects include:

photo courtesy Michigan DNR

Early example of a DNR Hummer conversion by the Roscommon Fire Experiment Station

- Coding of wildfire vehicles for aircraft identification
- Loading and tiedown procedures for tractors on tiltbed truck
- Fire chemical evaluation

Testing: The station's staff conducts testing of commercial equipment when appropriate. Early pumps, truck and track vehicles were the subject of many tests in the 1930's. New developments in pumps and vehicles (both wheeled and tracked) are continually tested for their suitability on forest fires.

Infrared scanners, direct current electric driven pumps, medium pressure-high volume pumps, commercial plows and tank units are among the items recently tested. These evaluations are necessary to make correct purchasing decisions, to develop specifications and to protect the taxpayer's dollars.

Roscommon Equipment Center Program: Since 1971, the Forest Fire Experiment Station has produced fire equipment designs, conducted research, and tested equipment for the twenty northeast states through a cooperative venture between the State of Michigan and the Northeast Forest Fire Supervisors under the banner "Roscommon Equipment Center" (REC).

Design plans of station developed equipment and evaluations have been distributed nation and worldwide through the REC project. Many projects published through the REC program incorporate the use of federal excess property vehicles, primarily multi-axle drive military units. This has helped foster the reutilization of these vehicles by rural and state fire agencies in an efficient and well engineered manner.

Other Cooperative Projects: Although built around and primarily concerned with fire related subjects, the station has done special work in other natural resource areas. Recent examples have included pesticide application systems for forest cultivation, cone tumbling units for forest nurseries, and transportation crates for relocating moose from Canada to Michigan's Upper Peninsula by air-truck transportation.[47]

☒ ☒ ☒ ☒ ☒

Brian Hutchins, present director of the Roscommon Fire Experiment Station recently noted that since its inception, the Station has had only three directors. Gil Stewart was the first, followed by Steve Such, and presently by Brian Hutchins who became director in 1984.

What the Press Has Had to Say About the Station

The Michigan Conservation magazine published an article in the January/February 1955 issue written by the first director of the DNR's Forest Fire Equipment Station, G.L. Stewart.

... Of Fires and Machines

Acres burned in 1908—2,300,000. Acres burned in 1954—3,384.

In a capsule, this is the success story of Michigan's down-through-the-years struggle against an ever lurking enemy, forest fire.

The struggle has been marked by steady improvement in techniques, personnel training, organization, communications and mechanized equipment. And not the least of these is mechanized equipment.

For the past 25 years the Michigan Department of Conservation has owned and operated modern machine shops at its Forest Fire Experiment Station at Roscommon. Here, highly specialized equipment is developed to do specific jobs in fire control.

A brief review of one current project at the station illustrates the usual course of development of practically all modern equipment.

During World War II, 4-wheel drive trucks were used successfully as military vehicles. New types and sizes had been produced, and following the war many of these models were placed on the market commercially. Smaller sizes of 4-wheel drive trucks satisfied field requirements for forest fire control equipment because of their capacity for off-the-road service. However, as purchased, they were usually stripped trucks, incorporating none of the accessories that would render them useful as woods equipment. The problem was to convert them into efficient units for forest fire control. In 1946, designs were created which equipped the first of these trucks as tanker units. High pressure pumps were used, and limited quantities of water were made very effective.

A whole new technique in fire control developed in Michigan which resulted in reduced fire losses, especially in the spring season. Continued use of 4-wheel drive trucks indicated further possible uses. It was demonstrated that their tractive capabilities approached those of crawler tractors. Subsequent experiments opened new possibilities and a very efficient type of fire control unit based on the 4-wheel drive truck was "invented."

As usual the entire project started solely in the idea stage, and considerable time elapsed before acceptable pilot models were produced. It was approached from the start as an engineering problem. The final machine was visualized as a truck tanker primarily, equipped with a small plowing unit and operated by hydraulic mechanisms. Design of tanker units themselves required little refinement, but the installation of plows on them was a new conception. Development work started in 1948 and took shape first on the drawing board. Active work was undertaken in the shops as designs were completed. Patterns were created to produce metal castings. Fabricated parts were developed. Accurate matching, welding and final assemblies were done as required, and tailor made pilot models were finally completed. At the same time installation of hydraulic equipment was being perfected for the trucks themselves.

Periods of extensive field testing followed. Corrections were made in design and certain parts made stronger as required. Refinements and improvements resulted, and the entire mechanism was simplified. This experimental period covered several years, but models of two successful units were perfected; one for truck mounting and one for use with crawler tractors. Production in quantity was authorized shortly afterward. Detailed drawings were finished and master specifications completed. Patterns, templates, fixtures, gauges, jigs, and all necessary tooling completed to assure uniform manufacture and quality control. Bills of material were assembled, and from these all materials were purchased. Twenty-nine complete truck and tractor units have now been built, incorporating the most modern equipment and accessories of the present day, complete with two-way radio system. They have been issued to field headquarters for use in forest fire control, and will serve that purpose for many years.

This process of inventing, developing, and manufacturing equipment is a day by day function of the experiment station. In winter and in summer the work goes on.

Thus it can be said that Michigan fights forest fires all year long. And the results?

Acres burned in 1908—2,300,000.

Acres burned in 1954—3,384.[48]

The previous article illustrates how the facility has progressed through the years from its inception. Following the war, they had little to work with, and in retrospect, they were setting standards. At that particular time, the completion of twenty-nine truck and tractor units was deemed remarkable. During that time frame, one of their four-wheel drive tanker-plow units could be operated by just one man, yet do the work of fifty men armed with shovels and backpack water units. It was indeed a giant step forward for the Department.

Progressing closer to modern times, the *Bay City Times* ran an excellent article written by Scott Harmsen, published August 7, 1988.

This Think Tank Exists to Experiment With Fire

ROSCOMMON—It's a low-key sort of place, a backwoods campus of warehouses, offices and shops.

A small wooden sign out front says "Forest Fire Experiment Station," but the searing violence of a raging wildfire seems miles away from this tranquil setting where field mice and chipmunks peacefully roam.

That's the way its supposed to be—because this place is intended for testing, experimenting and small-scale manufacturing of specialized forest firefighting equipment.

Unit manager Brian Hutchins has supervised the experiment station for more than five years.

A mechanical engineer, Hutchins said the station has three basic reasons for existence: equipment development, equipment testing and fire research.

Eleven people work at the station, including engineers, machinists, mechanics, welders, an office manager, draftsmen and a media development specialist who works with the station's newly installed television production studio and computerized publishing center.

A new computerized drafting system also has a place in the station's headquarters building.

When not working on product testing or development, the skilled craftsmen work on fabrication and repair of DNR fire line plows and water tanker units.

Despite the fact that the DNR's Region II headquarters is less than two miles away, the experiment station is actually a satellite of the Forest Management Division in Lansing—an arrangement that lets them work relatively undisturbed.

Hutchins said one of his most important functions at the station is to act as a buffer between the operation in the Northwoods and the bureaucracy in the capital.

The experiment station was created in 1929 as a cooperative venture between the Michigan Department of Conservation and the U.S. Forest Service. The two agencies each assigned a pair of men to the endeavor and built the pine-paneled grey concrete block building that still houses offices and shop areas.

Betty Sodders

Tractor/crawler with brush guards carried on a flat bed truck— DeTour field office, DNR Forestry Division

The station was given 6,000 acres of land—mostly jack pine forest that had reverted to the state for nonpayment of taxes—dedicated to forest fire research.

It's an appropriate site because jack pines are one of the greatest fire hazards in forest regions. Hutchins said there was a need for a center to study forest fire fighting because of the conflagrations that swept the Great Lakes states in the late 1800s and early 1900s.

"A lot of early fire research was done on the site," Hutchins said…Most of the present work at the Roscommon Equipment Center involves research and design reports on equipment. Many states now build firefighting equipment from designs developed at Roscommon, Hutchins said.

Test booklets produced at the station evaluate forest firefighting equipment and supplies. And although they don't normally respond to calls of forest fires, they do make prescribed test burns on station land.

…Bill Miller, supervisor of a U.S. Forest Service interregional professional firefighting crew from Bitterroot National Forest in Montana said the facilities' development of the Michigan fire plow makes life a lot easier when fighting fires in Michigan and states with similar terrain.

"Most people say it's the best of the fire line plows available," Hutchins said.

And the pride Hutchins displays when talking about the fire plow is exhibited throughout the shops and offices at the station.

Welder Don Duggar of Roscommon patiently explains how he fabricates 500 gallon water tanks from sheet steel.

"It's all fabricated here, everything but a valve and an elbow," he said.

Duggar, who has worked at the station for 5½ years, was preparing to paint a recently completed water tank with a new bright red elastic paint that is supposed to be more durable in the woods.

Machinist Pat Mattingly of Roscommon has worked at the station 10 years. Recently he was re-manufacturing fire plow latch parts on a milling machine.

"All the firefighting equipment of the state of Michigan comes out of here," he said as the machine quietly chewed curly-shaped metal shavings from a piece of steel.

Mattingly explained he is a tool and die maker by trade and worked for General Motors Corp. before heading north.

And although the station has evolved into a combination of testing ground, think tank and a custom manufacturing operation, the basic premise behind the facility remains the same: to generate better methods of combating forest fires and see that those improved methods come to fruition.[49]

There were other articles as well. One titled "The Michigan Story" appeared in the *Carling Conservation Digest* explored the history and work being performed at the facility.

A long, detailed, well-written feature story appeared in the September/October 1993 issue of *Michigan Natural Resources Magazine* written by Don Ingles and Brian Hutchins (the latter being the present director). An excerpt follows:

Like the Phoenix of legend, the FFES was born amid the ashes of the north's devastating wildfires, nurtured by the state's mechanical heritage, and has grown to be the national leader in forest fire equipment development. Using the station's equipment, the DNR's superbly trained forest fire officers have become a highly efficient force in taming the once uncontrollable wildfire problems. Integration of equipment and fire control tactics has made the Forest Fire Experiment Station and the state's fire control program inseparable. Thanks to forest fire control and more than 50 years of reforestation and modern forestry management, Michigan's forests are once more maturing, bringing economic importance to our state. A thriving tourism economy is also based on this valuable resource.

But times change and new problems arise. The influx of new residents into our forestlands has increased the wildfire risk for lives and property.

"Although we have made great strides in fire control in recent years we are not without danger," Hutchins said, "The recent and costly Stephan Bridge Fire, the Mack Lake Fire and the Seney Fire all show how dangerous the potential for wildfire remains today."

Brian Hutchins is realistic about potential wildfires in Michigan. "Catastrophic fires will happen here—that is the nature of our woodlands. But a small force stands ready with their machines to combat one of nature's mightiest forces, and a few more tinker in our shops building the best tools to help them meet the challenge."[50]

☒   ☒   ☒   ☒   ☒

In 1998, Dell Vaughn and Barry Stutzman of **The Michigan Magazine** public service TV show visited REC during the 19th Roscommon Mini-Equipment Workshop. Along with an interview with director Brian Hutchins, they showed some of the latest heavy duty firefighting equipment the center manufacturers and tests. The TV segment provided a fine group with credit due.

Chapter 12 of *Michigan on Fire 2* details the testing of the DNR's new Hummers. It illustrates their evaluation and testing methods.

A Brief Glimpse at Their Tanker Handbook

Following is a summary from the center's tanker handbook regarding military 5 ton 6x6 conversion. It is an excellent

photo courtesy Michigan DNR

Example of a REC 2.5 ton 10,000 gallon vehicle

example of the type of conversion work performed at the equipment center. This particular operator's manual provides tabulated data, operating precautions, warnings, operating instructions, functions, operational procedures, preventive maintenance checks and service info, inspections, troubleshooting guide plus a great deal more.

This catalog was published in December 1982, and updated September 1987.

REC Project No. 39–Military 5-Ton 6x6
1,500 Gallon, Low Profile Tanker

Background

The 5-ton, 6x6 military trucks are designed for use over all types of roads, highways, and cross country terrain. They will even ford hard bottom water crossings to depths of 30 inches. The most popular military configurations are dump trucks, tractor trucks and cargo trucks, though other special uses are made of this large and powerful prime mover.

The excellent cross country mobility of this vehicle makes it an outstanding candidate for forest fire control purposes, especially in potential use as a heavy duty tanker.

With its history of successful conversions into tankers of other military vehicles, the REC Committee in 1979 authorized the establishment of Project No. 39 to study the feasibility of designing a high volume tanker for the 5-ton 6x6. The study further included the actual fabrication of a 1500 gallon prototype tanker because design considerations proved positive. The first unit and new plans produced under this study was completed in April 1980 and immediately dispatched for fire duty and field testing.

Though not specifically mentioned in the initial project proposal, the first model was to include a medium-sized hydraulically operated fire line plow. The truck was also to be equipped with armor protection to guard against brush damage to glass and sheet metal truck parts.

With the advent of the 5-ton tanker, the entire popular family of mili-

R.E.C. Military 5-Ton 6x6
1,500 Gal. Low Profile Tanker Unit

Front View

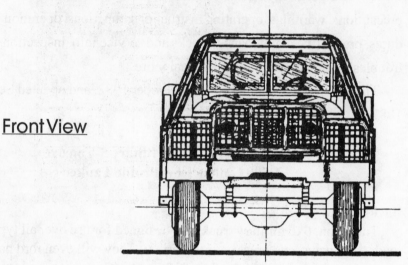

Top View

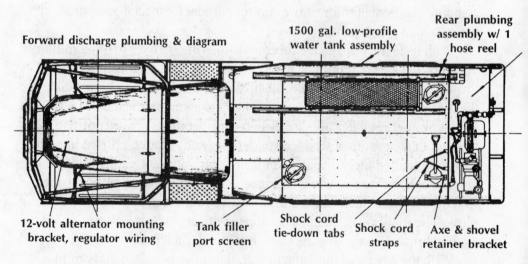

Forward discharge plumbing & diagram

1500 gal. low-profile water tank assembly

Rear plumbing assembly w/ 1 hose reel

12-volt alternator mounting bracket, regulator wiring

Tank filler port screen

Shock cord tie-down tabs

Shock cord straps

Axe & shovel retainer bracket

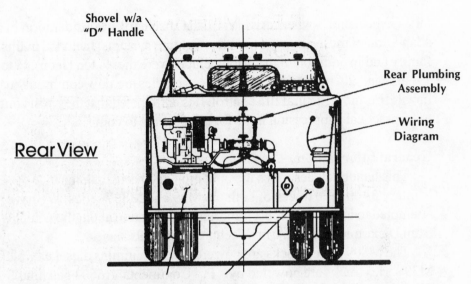

Shovel w/a "D" Handle

Rear Plumbing Assembly

Wiring Diagram

Rear View

Rear Compartments Door, Lock, & Sheet Metal Assembly

L.H. Profile View

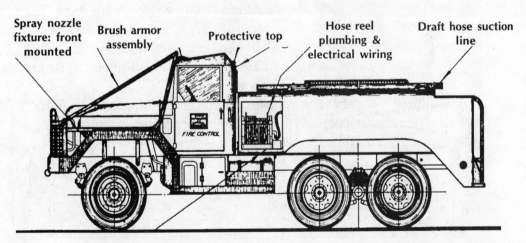

Spray nozzle fixture: front mounted

Brush armor assembly

Protective top

Hose reel plumbing & electrical wiring

Draft hose suction line

FIRE CONTROL

Forward compartment door & lock assembly

tary 4-wheel and 6-wheel drive trucks has been given consideration in the adaptation of these units to forest fire fighting systems. Included in this family and in addition to the 5-ton vehicle were the: ¼ ton (Jeep), ¾ ton, 1¼ ton, and 2¼ ton trucks. All of these vehicles are now commonly used in wildfire and structural fire control. It is anticipated that they will continue to be practical suppression units for many years to come.

General Information

This handbook describes the operation and basic maintenance of Military 5-ton, 6x6 trucks of both the M39 and M809 series. We have attempted to include the most important information about the vehicles from Department of the Army Technical Manuals.

The M809 series trucks are powered by a Cummins diesel engine. The M39 series trucks are powered by: (1) a Continental R6602 gasoline engine, (2) a Mack ENDT673 diesel engine, or (3) either a Continental 465-1 or LDS 465-1A multifuel engine. All are equipped with a manually operated, five-speed transmission and a two-speed transfer case which transmits power to front and rear axles. All are equipped with single front and dual rear tires. Service brakes are the air-activated, hydraulic type. The 5-ton truck is available with wheelbases of 167, 179, or 215 inches. Be sure you know the wheelbase length before starting fabrication of the tank unit, as the tank unit for each wheelbase will be slightly different. Refer to the drawings in the back of this handbook for details.

In addition to the above, several instruction and information plates are located on the instrument panel. They provide vehicle dimension, weight, shifting and other useful information.[51]

The Stephan Bridge Road Fire
1990

Details are furnished regarding one of Michigan's most disastrous modern-day forest fires that went on a fiery rampage before it could be subdued; its toll proved to be substantial.

In terms of fierceness, this fire was reminiscent of the days of Michigan's historic fires...but with one difference...fortunately, no lives were lost.

The Stephan Bridge Road Fire
1990

Case Study: Stephan Bridge Road Fire
Note: This study was prepared by the National Fire Protection Association, and sponsored by the National Wildland/Urban Interface Fire Protection Initiative.

Stephan Bridge Road Fire
May 8, 1990
Crawford County, MI
Destroyed:
76 Homes, 125 Other Structures, 37 Vehicles, 5,916 Acres

A rapidly spreading wildfire swept across 5,916 acres of a wildland/ urban interface area near Grayling, Michigan beginning around 3:50 P.M. on May 8, 1990.

More than 76 homes and 125 other structures, plus 37 vehicles and boats, were destroyed or heavily damaged during the approximately five hours in which the wind pushed the Stephan Bridge Road fire for a distance of more than eight miles. Losses from the fire have been estimated at $515 million, plus another $700,000 in destroyed timber. Extinguishment costs were more than $56,000. Due to a number of circumstances, 131 structures within the fire perimeter or immediately adjacent to it survived the fire.

The fire originated from the controlled burning of a large pile of brush and timber accumulated from recently cleared land. A burning permit was issued for the controlled burn and the burning was begun while snow covered the ground. It was later assumed that the pile was completely extinguished. However, investigators determined that the remaining fuel in the pile rekindled...seven weeks after that initial ignition...and escaped undetected from the cleared area. The resulting fire spread to other nearby ground fuels and extended into the adjacent forest before being detected by a Michigan Department of Natural Resources (DNR) aircraft pilot and observer.

Nature, especially weather, played a significant role in the ignition and spread of this fire. May is typically the month of highest weather-related fire danger in the region, a time when low rainfall, rising temperatures and high winds combine to dry out the forest and ground fuels.

Further affecting the conditions for severe fire danger were the soils in the region. With a high mixture of sand, the soil is quick to drain any precipitation, making it especially difficult for the growing vegetation to find moisture.

Deb Huff

Smoke billows high into the sky

…A cold front passed through the area around 8:30 that night. Strong gusting winds sent the fire out of control in a new direction, placing fire crews, evacuees and more homes in greater danger. Fortunately, the passing front also produced rainfall that helped contain the fire.

The predominate forest fuel in the area is "jack pine," which firefighters know during the early spring has characteristics that make it relatively easy to ignite and once ignited, produces fire intensity that results in rapid-spread crown fires…especially when driven by significant winds…and significant fire spotting.

First response to this fire was by the Michigan DNR. Some twenty-two fire departments and firefighters from local and state agencies worked to eventually contain the fire. Firefighters, law enforcement personnel and state employees combined to evacuate 500 residents from the fast-moving, wind-driven fire. Fortunately, there were no fatalities and only one firefighter was injured from smoke inhalation.

Findings from the analysis of this fire indicates that the initial scope and rate of spread of the fire was greater than could be controlled by human intervention. The Stephan Bridge Road fire burned through flat land where preheating of uphill fuels was not a factor. Up-slope winds and dry, combustible fuels are known to contribute to rapid fire spread in places such as Colorado and California, but the Stephan Bridge Road Fire reminds the homeowners and fire management personnel that combinations of several factors of terrain, weather, fuels and home construction can make homes susceptible to loss from wildfire in many other parts of the country as well.

The Local Landscape

The fire occurred in Crawford County, approximately nine miles east of Grayling, Michigan. Nearby state and local areas have much of the scenic beauty that is an important appeal of the wildland/urban interface. Lake Michigan lies less than 65 miles to the west, Lake Huron lies about 50 miles to the east, and the Mackinac Island resort area is less than 100 miles to the north. Closer to home, the AuSable River, world-famous for its trout fishing, flows through Crawford County. Numerous small lakes dot the region.

Crawford County is a four-seasons recreational area. Trout fishing, canoeing, skiing, hunting, hiking and snowmobiling are popular activities…the scenic forests are easily accessible, with about 70 percent of the county either state or federally owned.

In the wildland/urban interface areas of the county, about half of those who lost their homes and cabins were year-round residents.

…The AuSable River divides Grayling and extends northwest and east from town. Many homes have been built along the river on both sides. Because the AuSable was included in the state natural rivers program in 1987, any new (or rebuilt) structures must be moved back 200 feet from the stream's banks. About six miles east from town, Stephan Bridge crosses the river as a north-south link. State Highway 72 is to the south. North Down River Road, undeveloped wooded areas and various trails lie to the north. This connecting road is called the Stephan Bridge Road.

Regional Fire Activity, May 6–8, 1990

Fire danger conditions escalated dramatically in the region around Crawford County on May 6, when relative humidity dropped to 14 percent, the lowest reading of the days prior to the fire. On this day wind speed increased and fire fuel moisture dropped to a rating of 2 from a rating of 8 the day before, indicating that fallen leaves and other non-bulky surface fuels were very susceptible to continuous propagation from an ignition source.

The ratings soon translated into actual fires. May 7 saw the DNR responding to 21 wildfires in northern Lower Michigan. More than a third of them were in DNR District 7 alone. Staffing had been increased as the fire danger figures increased, according to established personnel policy.

photo courtesy Michigan DNR

A jack pine crowns

Equipment and personnel were at required standby stations and the fire management team members were on standby at Grayling. The DNR division office had been appraised of the fire conditions that morning. A DNR aircraft was patrolling, alert for quick detection of any fire. Everything was ready. Whatever else happened during the next several hours, neither delayed alarm nor delayed response would be contributing factors.

On May 7 a fire in the county burned within 200 yards of several large flammable liquid storage tanks. All of the fires were reported to be burning hot and fast, with excessive spotting. Winds and heat continued to dry out the fuels.

By the afternoon of May 8 there were 15 more wildfires being worked by the DNR in the region, and more personnel were involved with the careful but time-consuming mop-up needed on many of the fires from the previous day. Again, more than a third of these new fires were in DNR District 7 alone. The USDA Forest Service and local fire departments responded to many additional fires in those two days that are not counted here.

As in the major fire history of the past 25 years in the area in and adjacent to Crawford County, the multiple fires of May 7 and 8 were not ignited from natural causes. People were responsible. Debris burning was the most common single cause. Accidents involving mechanical equipment was the next in frequency.

Because of the fires and the continuing danger, a DNR airplane was on patrol May 8. At 3:40 P.M. the pilot detected a fire near McMasters Bridge, 14 miles east of Grayling. Similar to the area of the subsequent Stephan Bridge Road fire, the McMasters Bridge area featured dense jack pine, so several units responded, including a fire management team. Units from Mio to the east and Roscommon to the south were dispatched because this was a high-hazard zone fire with homes in danger. Some of the personnel and equipment responded from their standby location at North Down River Road and McMasters Bridge Road.

Circling in the area at 3:53 P.M., the DNR airplane saw smoke from a new fire ten miles back towards Grayling from the McMasters Bridge. The new fire was a mile west of Stephan Bridge Road and just north of Michigan Highway 72. Additional personnel responding to the McMasters Bridge fire were redirected to what became the more-serious Stephan Bridge Road fire. A tractor-plow also responded from the Grayling field station.

Most of the fires in the region on May 7 and 8 were caught quickly and held to a relatively small number of acres burned. From the first moments it was obvious that the Stephan Bridge Road fire was going to be bigger than the others.

During the attack on this fire, at 5:06 P.M., yet another major local fire was reported along the same Stephan Bridge Road. Named the Billman fire, it was nine miles to the south, requiring more equipment and personnel to be diverted. Here, too, homes and outbuildings were threatened, and several were lost. This fire was also to cause confusion in the radio communications because both fires were related to Stephan Bridge Road, although miles apart. The Billman Road fire eventually burned 615 acres and took five homes and 15 outbuildings. Numerous cars, boats, motorhomes and off-road vehicles were also lost.

Regional Fire History

DNR records of 11 major wildfires...not counting the Stephan Bridge Road fire in Crawford and three adjacent counties during the last 25 years show certain trends.

Windy afternoons in May with low relative humidity are obviously high risk periods.

Natural causes, such as lightning, caused none of the fires; people did.

The average number of acres burned in 10 of the major fires was 1,350. A football field is approximately one acre in size.

The additional notable fire in regional history, the Mack Lake fire, burned about 25,000 acres, with the major fire spread occurring in an 8-hour period...noon to 8:00 P.M.[52]

Eyewitness Reports: Stephan Bridge Fire

The following eyewitness reports were gleaned from the Stephan Bridge Road Fire Case Study prepared by the National Fire Protection Association, Quincy, Massachusetts. All accounts were taken from newspaper reports.

Witness: John Murray said he had been told for years that the surrounding jack pines were prime candidates for a devastating forest fire, but he told a reporter after the fire that he never believed it.

His home was destroyed…

Witness: "It's like losing a member of the family," said Horton, a Flint carpenter who built the cabin in 1947 with his father and planned to pass it along to his sons. "We have been coming up, summer and winter, since

photo courtesy Michigan DNR

A trio of firemen and a hose battle the Stephan Bridge Road Fire

they were little boys. Our place was like a museum. I'm a great collector...license plates, beer bottles, all kinds of antiques. There were deer hides and trophy heads.

"Are we going to rebuild? Don't talk to me about rebuilding. I'm 65 years old."   —Dick Horton, remembering his cedar-sided
                    three-bedroom cottage, one of the first to burn.

Witness: "In all the 37 years I've been around house fires in Grayling, I saw more houses burn today than all the other years combined."
        —Sheriff Harold Hatfield

Witness: "It was the scariest fire I've ever been in. It was the most houses I've ever seen burn in my 27 years of firefighting."
        —Ed Holtcamp, Beaver Creek Fire Chief

Witness: "If the rains had not come and the winds died down as they did, the fire would have probably burned through the night and taken off and run all day the next day."
        —Duane Brooks, DNR fire officer

Witness: "I never believed a fire could move that fast. The smoke was so thick the sun was just a dim, red ball."
        —Julie Gates, wife of Rusty Gates, owner of AuSable Lodge

Witness: Jonathan Weymers, 21, had gone downstate to pick up a bed. He returned with his wife and daughter to find that everything except the bed had been destroyed by the fire. They did not have any insurance.[53]

A special edition containing fire news, related stories, and photographs was printed by the *Crawford County Avalanche* that more or less brought the Stephan Bridge Fire to light for its readers.

Crawford County Avalanche, special edition, May 10, 17, 24, 31

Fire Losses Hit $3.5 Million

The most destructive forest fire in Crawford County history swept through the area on Tuesday, May 8, destroying homes and outbuildings valued at nearly $3.5 million. The DNR said the fire was started by "human activity."

Miraculously, the only fire related injury reported was smoke inhalation by a fireman who was treated and released from Mercy Hospital. The injury occurred during the evacuation effort when the fireman pushed open a door and was met with a thick cloud of black smoke.

…DNR Fire Officer Duane Brooks said the fire could be the most expensive forest fire in Michigan's history. He said the fire appeared to have started off Thendara Road and burned out of control from about 3:56 to 11 P.M. The fire traveled in a northeasterly direction for about nine miles jumping Stephan Bridge Road just south of the bridge, the AuSable River at Guides Rest, and North Down River Road twice before it was contained in a swampy area near Dyer Trail. It was finally extinguished by heavy rains on Tuesday.

Governor James Blanchard declared the county a disaster area at about 10:50 P.M. on Tuesday and he and DNR David Hales visited the burned area on Wednesday afternoon. Designation as a disaster area will allow victims to apply for state aid to help with reconstruction efforts.

DNR firefighting units from all over northern and north central Michigan were called in to battle the blaze. Volunteer fire departments from surrounding counties, as well as every fire department in Crawford County assisted in the firefighting effort. The Michigan National Guard fire unit assisted with men and equipment. An Ohio National Guard helicopter crew fought the fire with their Bambi Bucket until additional helicopters could be flown in by the Michigan National Guard. Eventually three buckets were used to carry water to the fire.

Crawford County Sheriff Dept. was assisted by the Michigan State Police, military MP's, and sheriff departments from several neighboring counties. Conservation officers were called in from all over northern Michigan.

About 150 persons worked together to evacuate the area, contain the fire, and control traffic. Equipment at the fire included 73 tractors/plows and water units.

More than 300 persons were evacuated Tuesday afternoon. Shelter was provided at the Michelson Memorial United Methodist Church, the Grayling High School gymnasium and Camp Grayling. Some stayed with friends.

Residents were allowed to return to the evacuated area about 4 P.M. on Wednesday afternoon. Some residents complained because they had been kept out of the area 17 hours after the fire had been contained, but Brooks said this was necessary to allow the electric utilities time to cut power to all downed electric wires and to ensure there was no further danger of propane gas tank explosions.

Many of those who had been evacuated returned to find their homes as they had left them, but others found only ash where their homes once stood.[54]

☒　　☒　　☒　　☒　　☒

Other Statewide Headlines Read:

South Branch Fire Burns 615 Acres...Losses at $500,000

Community Support Poured In

Red Cross Still Offering Assistance to Fire Victims

Fire Destroys At Least 50 Homes..."I saw 14 houses burning in a single block in the Shaw Park area." —Firefighter Dean Goss

Rain Helped Knock Down Fire

March 16th Brush Pile Burn Re-ignited to Start Forest Fire

What Comes Next in Aftermath of Fire?

Some Residents Will Rebuild

photo courtesy Michigan DNR

A volunteer firefighter throws clods of dirt on the fire, holding the line

Landowners Faced With Tough Choices About Burned Timber

County Declared Disaster Area

Hell's Fury

Buildings In Clearings Fared Batter

Crawford County is Filled With Wonderful, Caring People

☒　☒　☒　☒　☒

One article by Jon Thompson and Irene Pettyjohn touches on a subject not yet addressed in detail.

Fire Destroys At Least 50 Homes

The most expensive forest fire in Crawford County's history burned out of control from 3:58 P.M. Tuesday, May 8, until about 11 P.M. when most of the blaze was contained.

Firefighters estimated more than 50 houses burned to the ground in an area from Thendara Rd., northeast to Stephan Bridge Rd., Shaw Rd., Pine Rd., and North Down River Rd., to Bald Hill Rd. Damages were initially estimated at $2.4 million by county equalization director Bill Borchers. At 9:55 P.M. Governor Blanchard declared it a disaster area.

DNR firefighter Duane Brooks said the fire produced more monetary loss than the large Mack Lake fire a couple years ago. "It was the scariest fire I've ever been in," said Beaver Creek Fire Chief Ed Holtcamp.

Strong winds pushed the blaze northeast quickly from Pappy's Trail, where the fire started.

"This was the worst fire I've fought because of the wind," said Howard Taylor, a firefighter with the DNR crew for 15 years.

Only two persons were listed as injured from the fire…two firefighters… as of midnight Tuesday. DNR Conservation officers, Sheriff deputies, and other law enforcement personnel evacuated 300–400 persons from the fire area.

Among some of the homes that were destroyed or close to the fire's path were Carl Youst's, Jay Stephan's, Del Kuck's, and RoxAnn Adam's.

Officer Dean Goss, who is also the assistant fire chief for the Grayling City and Township Fire Dept., said the destruction was unbelievable. Goss said many homes on Pine Road and both sides of North Down River Road were lost. He said the first house that burned was on Pappy's Trail.

"There is no way to take an accurate count of the homes and cabins burned," said Goss. "We evacuated about 300 people."

The fire path jumped around. One house on Stephan Bridge Rd. did not burn while houses on each side burned. Garages and outbuildings burned at Mike and Beth Wieland's but their house did not. That happened in several places.

...Problems firefighters ran into were crown fires (fires racing among the tops of trees), power lines falling, and propane tanks exploding. About 1,400 Top of Michigan customers lost power because of downed lines.

Beth Wieland was at her home trying to gather up a few items before the fire came.

"It came down the power line and it sounded like a train coming," she said. "The heat and smoke were so bad we had to leave."

Police had trouble evacuating people. Some were refusing to leave the danger area. Other people were causing problems at the roadblocks and one man was arrested for carrying a weapon. As the firefighters began getting a handle on the blaze, reports of people looting in the evacuated areas started coming into the central dispatch office at the sheriff dept.

People throughout Grayling pulled together during the tragedy. Motels offered lodging; restaurants and grocery stores offered food and items to firefighters and evacuated people. Camp Grayling opened its doors to the evacuated people for the night.

As the *Crawford County Avalanche* went to press early Wednesday morning, DNR firefighters were planning on meeting at the Command Center set up at Duane LaMotte's Down River Pines store at the intersection of M-72 East and Stephan Bridge Rd. early Wednesday morning for the next step.

Firefighters were concerned another dry, windy day would start up smoldering fires.

Other Area Fire Fires:

The second week in May is an historic week for forest fires in northern Michigan. On May 8, 1968, fires in Beaver Creek and South Branch townships burned over 6,000 acres. On May 10, 1975, 3,598 acres burned in the Bald Hill area and an additional 2,802 acres burned on North Down River Road. More than 25,000 acres were destroyed in the Mack Lake, Mio fire on May 5, 1980, and 1,931 acres were lost in Ogemaw County during the Damon Fire on May 9, 1987.[55]

The Aftermath

Detroit Free Press, Monday June 25, 1990
Byline: James Ricci

Venerable Natives Surrender to Flame

GRAYLING—They auctioned some damaged goods recently at the DNR's district field office. Clipboard-carrying men in ball caps and flannel shirts—timber producers, most of them—bid on the leavings of last month's forest fire.

No one is crazy about handling charred timber; it's a mess. On the other hand, the price is right. In an hour, almost 1.9-million board feet of sawlogs and more than 10,000 cords of pulp wood sold for $123,000 and change, perhaps a quarter of what the timber would have commanded undamaged.

The ultimate office sale. Short-lived humans' hapless response to an event that will drastically alter 5,432 acres of woodland for longer than the auctiongoers, and in some cases their children' will live.

photo courtesy Michigan DNR

All agencies responded to the Stephan Road Bridge Fire; here fire-equipped DNR vehicles respond in readiness

Geographically, it was not a monstrous fire. But more and more people had come to live in the woods of Crawford County, and the blaze devoured 86 residences. Some owners stayed by their houses and watched as a first wave of wind-driven flames raced past, searing their property. Then, when they'd scarcely emptied their homes in relief, a subsequent wave scattered them in flight and pounced on what had been "saved." Fortunately, no lives were lost. A rough estimate of damage is $6.5 million.

"In terms of people's loss, this was one hell of a big fire," said DNR silviculturist Bill Mahalak, "Probably the biggest since the early 1900s."

Houses, at least, unlike forests, can be rebuilt in a few months.

There is an eeriness, a surrealistic wintriness, in much of the 8-mile-long crescent the fire branded into the land's hide. Powerful aroma of wood char permeates the air. Crooked, blackened branches are strewn at the feet of the standing dead.

The fire began on May 8 around 3:30 P.M. when high winds licked flames to life in a secretly smoldering pile of brush a mile east of Stephan Bridge Road. Sputtered by the winds of a cold front, the blaze sped down

photo courtesy Michigan DNR

The aftermath—time for mopping-up

Chapter 11
The Stephan Bridge Road Fire
1990

North Down River Road. It leapt across the pavement and back again several times, covering eight miles in five hours. Then, around 8:40 P.M., a god-gift of rain fell for 15 minutes. The winds calmed. DNR firefighters brought the beast to heel 100 yards from a stand of 170-year-old red pines Mahalak called "the best example of old-growth red pine in the state."

Still, the fire took many trees older than old men. In the burned crescent, Mahalak can trace the fire's footprints. Here is where it crawled along the ground, here where it ascended the branches, here where it flew in abandon from treetop to treetop. Islands of black amid green trees, these are where firebrands hurled by the blaze caused ancillary burning.

Where the fire burned especially hot, it consumed leaves and forest-floor litter and bared the mineral soil beneath. Elsewhere, needles burned red-brown and deciduous leaves singed to tan twitch dryly on trees that were more gently cooked.

Sparks of life.

Sedge grass and bracken fern have already regrown ankle height in many places. Thorough transformations of some plots are inexorably under way.

In one tract, 80-year-old red pines 65 feet tall stand coated in place. The trees' cones are not mature till autumn. The fire caught the pines in a moment of virtual unproductibility. On the other hand, small burned oaks that grow in the shadow of the pines have already sent up red shoots from buds three inches beneath the soil, where fire did not harm them. Nurtured by powerful old roots, these will reach a height of five feet in a year or two. In other words, oak will prevail here. The stateliness of red pine will not return.

Ironically, the forest stands its best chance of regenerating in places that were burned worst. To demonstrate, Mahalak goes to an incinerated stand of jack pines. The fire melted the resin that had kept the trees' cones closed. As the cones dried and their scales contracted in the first days after the fire, they showered tiny seeds onto the earth, which had been burned clean of sedge that might have contested the seeds' germination.

And, in 50 or 60 years, presto, another stand of mature jack pine. Too bad I likely won't be around to see it.[56] *(Reprinted by permission of the Detroit Free Press)*

A Look at Michigan's DNR Fire-Equipped Humvees

Humvees or Hummers serve an important role in the fighting of certain types of forest fires. This chapter details the facts: How they are equipped...What types of jobs they perform...How many the DNR currently maintains...How much they cost...Why that cost is justified.

My tour in a fire-equipped DNR Hummer simply sold me on this unique piece of valued equipment.

Hummers
A Look At Michigan's DNR Fire-Equipped Humvees

HUMMER: Fire Truck Chassis

- 300 gallon water tank
- Pump capacity of 64 gpm at 150 PSI
- Foam injection system
- Two front bumper-mounted water nozzles
- Water run located in cab
- Two ¾ inch diameter 1000 foot hose lines
- Drafting line to fill tank and other trucks
- Engine: GM 6.2-L Diesel
- Horsepower: 150 hp @ 3600 rpm

Humvees find a niche in civilian life. The Humvee name is an acronym derived from Army jargon—High Mobility Multipurpose Wheeled Vehicle. Civilian models are called Hummers.

To the Michigan Department of Natural Resources, Forest Service Division, Hummers are not revamped military issue. They are brand new machines, built to MDNR specifications by AM General Corporation of South Bend, Indiana. AM General has been building the Hummer since 1984. The company has manufactured more than 100,000 of the vehicles for armed service demand. The Humvee replaced the popular military jeep. It earned its reputation for toughness and durability during the Persian Gulf conflict. It proved to be the backbone of the U.S. Army's land assault in the desert.

Each Hummer cost $60,000 including chassis and conversion by the contractor for fire usage. Primarily designed for initial attack, they can also support tractor-plows along a fireline, and perform general mop-up duties.[57]

While the MDNR Hummer is somewhat limited by terrain or ground pressure, its high ground clearance and special driveline characteristics allow it to climb hills and traverse off-road situations better than most wheeled vehicles, which tend to perform poorly in swamps, bogs, or marshy areas.

"All vehicles have pros and cons," remarked Brian Hutchins, Supervisor at Michigan's DNR Forest Fire Experimental Station, Roscommon, "The Hummers have a greater load capacity than standard pickup trucks, but smaller than medium duty truck chassis. Each have their roles in firefighting. The Hummer units combine maneuverability, high ground clearance and a low center of gravity. The last two items are difficult to achieve together. That is what makes this vehicle unique."

"Two of our Hummers have central tire inflation, which allows the operator to adjust tire pressure to match driving conditions. All are equipped with foam proportioners and carry water tanks."[58]

Hummers are 85 inches wide—more than seven feet. This fact often takes people by surprise. The width of an average traffic lane is twelve feet, thus, minus rearview mirrors, the operator has approximately 2½ feet of leeway on either side.

Standard highway trucks (semis) are 96 inches wide. Pickup trucks are under 80 inches wide. Hence they are slightly wider than a pickup. They are easy to drive but require some training to drive effectively off road. In certain situations the driver uses brake modulation to gain traction. This means the operator can virtually lock up or assure no slippage of a wheel by gently riding the brake, while applying power.

All Michigan DNR Hummers are diesel fueled and maintain a ratio of 12–16 mpg highway; 8–14 mpg off road. It is surprising how the engine affords a rugged rumble; it is not quite as smoothly quiet as a gasoline motor, nevertheless, it is capable of moving the vehicle from 0 to 60 mph in close to 18 seconds.[59]

Betty Sodders
DNR Hummer outside the Sault Ste. Marie DNR field office

John Krzycki, Assistant Area Resource Protection Fire Supervisor, Sault Ste. Marie DNR field office, afforded your author a field trial of this remarkable firefighting, off road vehicle.

Part of Krzycki's job is to train fire personnel in the driving skills needed to operate this machine. During our tour, John took the Hummer through various off road situations while explaining how and why the vehicle was responding.

As we crossed a rough field reverting back to nature, John's coffee mug was sitting on the wide console between the vehicle's two bucket seats. Had we crisscrossed this type of furrowed terrain in my standard-sized 4x4 pickup, we surely would have jostled about, but not in the Hummer. And that cup of Java never spilled one drop! Furthermore, I was taking notes with pad and pen just as though we were back at the field office interviewing Krzycki while sitting behind his desk.

Our next test was to work several low ridges at a county-owned gravel pit. John remarked that a Hummer can easily manage a 45° angle climb or downgrade, and under certain circumstances, could maneuver a grade as steep as 60°. John Krzycki has devised a training course located at Kinross, southwest of the Sault. "Here," he stated, "at times some trainees are ready to bail out until they get the feel of what this machine can safely handle."

When an obstacle such as a downed tree, log or rock is encountered, it must be angle approached which allows each wheel to singly traverse that obstruction. To further demonstrate, Krzycki approached a log at the required angle and the unit nicely climbed over it with the front left wheel, then the right, followed by the back left wheel, finally the right. Little effort expended!

Next, a rock under the specified 18 inch height level proved to be our target. In this instance, the two driver's side wheels were involved. Once more, we simply angled into the rock while the Hummer performed its assigned task.

Another type of terrain John demonstrated was one in which you could possibly be straddling a deep ditch with two wheels firmly on ground. Here, two left side wheels pulled, while the right wheels rode on little more than free air space.

During our trial run, John explained the theory of modulation. With the driver's foot lightly placed on the brake, and using appropriate gears, each of the Hummer's wheels gained traction independently. Should the vehicle become mud mired, modulation would be employed. The vehicle's occupants would feel the machine "jump" from a stuck position as though a "come- along" were being used. Through a series of modulation maneuvers, the stuck vehicle would literally pull itself free.

I asked Krzycki why his fire-equipped Hummer had brush guards and was informed the department installed them for protection. In firefighting work, narrow two-tracks are often traversed; due to the Hummer's wide stance, small saplings can easily whip backward resulting in possible window breakage. John also noted that MDNR supports a policy that Hummers will not be driven with windows rolled down; saplings thrust through a window opening are capable of causing severe injury or death to driver or passenger. For this reason, all forest service department Hummers have been equipped with air conditioning.

The quick maneuverability of these unusual firefighting units was demonstrated as we drove along a narrow truck trail. With a quick twist of his wrist, John flicked the small-sized steering wheel, turning the Hummer to avoid an unexpected obstacle. One moment we were headed straight ahead; next, the Hummer turned sharply—not unlike a mustang cutting cattle.

Even the Hummer's radio is extraordinary. John explained how all DNR District Four transmissions could be picked up. When entering District Three, a mere twist of his finger brought that frequency into play. The same holds true for all downstate DNR districts (Michigan's Upper Peninsula is divided into four districts while lower Michigan contains nine).

A Look at Michigan's DNR Fire-Equipped Humvees

While we tooled along, I asked Krzycki if his Hummer attracts attention. "It surely does," he commented, "but when folks see this unit traveling a remote stretch of highway during the dark of night with my wig-wag lights turned on, hey, I've been told that the Hummer appears to be only two feet tall and as wide as a house; folks are left scratching their heads wondering what they just saw!"

During the winter of 1995–96, a blizzard hard-hit the Sault area with six feet of snow that fell over a single weekend. Krzycki's DNR Hummer was pressed into service as a rescue unit running Highway M-129 and Interstate I-75 for the sole purpose of aiding stranded motorists.

Krzycki has trained over twenty drivers in the art of operating one of these firefighting off road vehicles. One of the first things he does is to have a trainee place his left (braking) foot securely between the Hummer's seat and door, so the new driver will be less tempted to

Betty Sodders

John Krzycki, DNR Assistance Area Resource Protection Fire Supervisor, Sault Ste. Marie, Michigan, showing off the reeled hose of the Hummer

employ the brake when traveling off road terrain. The brake is never used except during modulation. However, braking remains standard procedure during highway travel.[60]

When our field trip finished, I was completely sold on the abilities of this compact forest firefighting vehicle that could go just about anywhere it was needed.

During a follow up interview with Gregory Lusk, Upper Peninsula Resource Protection Manager, at the DNRs Marquette office, I learned that the department has a total of thirteen fire- equipped Hummers on the force. These units are stationed at: Gwinn, Stephenson, and Sault Ste. Marie (Upper Peninsula); Pellston, Gaylord, and Platte River (northern lower Michigan); Harrison, Baldwin, Oceana, Cass City, Muskegon, Brighton, and Yankee Springs (southern lower Michigan).[61]

It bothered me that more than half the Hummers were positioned at extreme lower Michigan facilities when the heavily forested areas of the state occupy most of northern Michigan and the entire U.P. The answer proved to be threefold: Budget necessities, type of terrain the vehicle would be obliged to work in, and the Hummer's distinctive capabilities.

Like any homeowner balancing a personal budget, Michigan Forest Fire Division managers must evaluate specific needs and priorities within a set amount of available funds. The process begins as district fire supervisors petition their immediate needs, then the resource protection manager lists his top priorities gleaned from these requisitions. Finally, requests are placed before a Michigan DNR Equipment Board that meets in June at the Roscommon Experimental Fire Station Headquarters.

Budget needs of the Upper Peninsula along with northern Michigan prove far more diverse than those of mid/southern Michigan. Budget allotments represent a spread of items—a laundry list, so to speak. Money is sorely lacking. Many firefighting engines and pumper trucks are passing the twenty year mark; parts are nearly impossible to obtain. Concentration of just one type of firefighting equipment could prove foolhardy.

Terrain plays a major role in Hummer placement. For example, the heavily forested sections found north of Newberry (Upper Peninsula) along the Tahquamenon watershed, requires large load carrying capacity tanker trucks. Hummers do not perform well in this type of situation; water availability remains a prime requisite. Hummers carry a 300 gallon capacity that is increased through foam proportioners. The big rigs contain far more.

Hummers stationed at Stephenson (western U.P. near the Wisconsin border) and at Sault Ste. Marie (eastern end of the Upper Peninsula), were so positioned as to serve cropland situations interspersed with forested sections that contained heavy clay soils. Conventional forest firefighting equipment bogs down in clay; Hummers adapt adequately.

The Hummer unit assigned to Gwinn (central U.P.) is well-equipped to meet the worst type of hazard fuel, that being a jack pine forest. Pines burn like a torch—very hot—quickly. Fires crown from standing pine to standing pine. Parts of northern lower Michigan also contain they type of volatile habitat and Hummers have been assigned accordingly.

The third factor of the equation remains: the Hummer is considered a "quick entry," "fast exit" vehicle, capable of adequately containing small wildfires from becoming a major blaze. They prove ideal where population intrusions bring high fire danger in country living settings.

In conclusion, the Hummer with its low center of gravity is easy to maneuver so that it can take field operators quickly into a fast spreading forest fire situation, well before it erupts into an emergency. Hummers accomplish the job they were designed for—and do it exceedingly well!

Roscommon Equipment Center Evaluates The DNR Hummer

Michigan's Forest Fire Experimental Station located at Roscommon evaluated the Hummer and HMMWV Series Chassis for wildland engine use. This study, Project Number 56, September 1993, analyzed the U.S. Military M-998 series and its similar commercial models, known as the HUMMER, for use as wildland fire engines.

In the early 1980's, AM General Corporation designed what came to be known as the "High Mobility, Multi Purposed, Wheeled Vehicle" (HMMWV) for the U.S. Military. The M998 Cargo Troop Carrier is the base unit of this group. These vehicles succeeded the M151 Jeep, M880's and Gama-Goat. At a 1988 meeting between wildfire agency and truck manufacturer representatives, AM General showed a desire to make the HUMMER available to fire fleets. The Roscommon Equipment Center (REC) program also had an interest to evaluate this vehicle anticipating future availability through Federal Excess Personal Property. In 1989, the State of Michigan and AM General reached agreement which provided the Michigan Department of Natural Resources a HUMMER for evaluation. Michigan made the first purchase of such a unit. In 1992 AM General began offering the commercial version for public sale.

Design and prototype production of the fire package was done by the staff at the Michigan Forest Fire Experiment Station. The prototype went through three seasons of field evaluations, primarily in Michigan. Some evaluation was made in Nevada and Idaho, in conjunction with the USDI Bureau of Land Management (BLM). While built from the same base unit, the commercial HUMMER and the military HMMWV have some basic differences.

To evaluate the commercial HUMMER prototype, REC staff designed and built the wildland fire vehicle with the following goals:

1: Design a prototype wildland fire engine. Primary use; initial attack unit

2: Test the PRIMER chassis in wildland field trials at full GVWR.

Adaptations and test results were drawn together in the following Summary that appears in the project 56 booklet:

Summary: REC is well familiar with the current line up of commercial 4x4 (pickup) trucks. The AM General HUMMER was evaluated in part to compare its performance to that of the commercial pickup chassis; there is little comparison. With the constant full load situation of a fire vehicle, we believe the life expectancy of the HUMMER will be at least twice that of a commercial 1-ton 4x4. The water capacity will also be approximately twice

Betty Sodders

A view of the Hummer's "wide stance" while garaged

as much. The mobility and off-road performance, primarily because of the HUMMER's underbody clearance, will be much more than other vehicles of its size. But, these come at a price: the user will pay twice the cost for the basic chassis.

The user should be aware of the differences between the commercial HUMMER and military HMMWV chassis. Besides having a 12-volt electrical system and a sedan style cab, the commercial unit has differences in power train, springs, and body construction to increase its payload. Those converting military vehicles to fire units should heed the BVWR labels for that vehicle. Fire apparatus designed to fully utilize a commercial HUMMER unit will overload most military units.

Our test HUMMER was utilized primarily as an initial attack water unit. It also had utility as an off-road mop-up unit, by combining the 300 gallon water capacity with a Class A foam system. It was excellent for use as a patrol vehicle and for carrying supplies in off-road situations.

The low profile design made this vehicle extremely stable and allowed it to drive underneath many tree canopies and obstructions. Military studies found that the HUMMER could traverse significantly more terrain than its predecessor Jeep, M-880 or Commercial Utility Cargo Vehicle. The radial tires and CTIS on our test unit enhanced the mobility over standard bias ply military HMMWVs.

Despite its design for off-highway performance, this vehicle performed more than adequately on the highway. It is probably the best lightweight off-highway wheeled vehicle available today. In many ways, it reminds us of the Dodge Power Wagon of old. The 1960 vintage Power Wagons are still used by many as the yardstick of what a forest fire control vehicle should be. The capacity of the commercial HUMMER rivals that of the old Power Wagon. Its maneuverability and off-highway performance is better than that of the Power Wagon. We expect its durability to compare very favorably. The differences come mostly in style and space available for placing equipment.

While for many agencies, initial chassis cost will be a definite negative factor, the HUMMER comes highly recommended, based on our experience, for the tasks listed above.[62]

Conclusion

Spring 1998: Held Highest Fire Danger in Years

Generally speaking, we probably regard the forest fire season as taking place during the hottest parts of the summer, but in essence the months of April and May prove far more dangerous, prior to green-up when hot weather is followed by snow loss. With below normal snowfall, an early dry spring afforded 1998 a "high fire danger" status throughout the entire state.

State fire crews responded to 133 fires during the spring compared to 96 the previous season. The dry conditions were evident in the fact that 133 fires burned almost 1,000 acres, while the number of acres burned at this time in 1997 numbered 400.

Forty Michigan counties experienced spring wild fires during 1998, caused by: burning debris, smoking, power lines, children, stove ashes, electric fences, equipment, campfires, railroads, cutting tools, and a number of suspicious and/or incendiary blazes (see 1998 Michigan Wildfires–DNR Listing Sheet on page 177).

A thirty-acre fire near Lovells required several homes to be evacuated as fire advanced throughout the jack pine forest. Quick action by firefighters and the single engine Air Tanker stopped the fire before it reached any structures. That particular fire started by someone burning a pile of debris.

A similar incident occurred in Marquette County when equipment started a conflagration that burned across 224 acres.

A devastating fire erupted in Chippewa County near Raco that burned over 1,000 acres before suppression.

Rain eased the fire danger somewhat across northern lower Michigan during the second week in May, thus the Air Tanker and six firefighters were shifted to the Upper Peninsula to assist in fire possibilities there.

photo courtesy Michigan DNR

Fire in Progress

Michigan Forest Fires
as recorded by Michigan Department of Natural Resources

YEAR	FIRES	ACRES BURNED	AVERAGE
1950	873	5,606	6.4
1951	670	4,491	6.7
1952	1,624	12,864	7.9
1953	1,475	11,191	7.6
1954	1,010	8,884	8.8
1955	1,154	7,143	6.2
1956	702	3,420	4.9
1957	743	6,355	8 5
1958	1,251	11,992	9.6
1959	726	3,713	5.1
1960	517	2,978	5.8

MICHIGAN ON FIRE 2

YEAR	FIRES	ACRES BURNED	AVERAGE
1961	1,142	8,176	7.1
1962	746	6,267	8.4
1963	1,303	9,269	7.1
1964	1,227	18,108	14.7
1965	777	2,885	3.7
1966	1,672	13,691	8.2
1967	868	2,884	3.3
1968	1,185	16,333	13.7
1969	1,016	6,544	6.4
1970	1,393	6,367	4.6
1971	1,210	5,593	4.6
1972	1,060	5,646	5.3
1973	832	2,664	3.2
1974	1,035	6,107	5.9
1975	853	16,796	19.6
1976	1,341	25,470	18.9
1977	1,433	12,109	8.4
1978	721	2,639	3.6
1979	472	2,293	4.8
1980	842	9,423	11.2
1981	832	7,694	9.2
1982	483	4,135	8.6
1983	547	4,374	8.0
1984	613	4,070	6.6
1985	357	3,112	8.7
1986	493	9,712	19.7
1987	832	9,585	11.5
1988	1,095	8,049	7.3
1989	710	4,560	6.4
1990	483	9,157	18.9
1991	412	1,473	3.5
1992	552	1,976	3.5
1993	231	893	3.8
1994	546	5,040	9.2
1995	554	4,395	7.9
1996	350	2,140	6.1
1997	503	1,566	3.11

1998 Michigan Wildfires

County	Acres Burned	Cause	County	Acres Burned	Cause
Alcona	.3 acres	power line	Dickinson	10 acres	debris burning
	.2 acres	power line		8 acres	stove ashes
	3 acres	debris burning		.8 acre	debris burning
	.3 acres	power line	Gladwin	.5 acre	debris burning
	1 acre	campfire		25 acres	campfire
	33 acres	debris burning	Grand	3 acres	children
	23 acres	smoking	Traverse	2 acres	campfire
	2 acres	debris burning	Houghton	.1 acre	debris burning
	.5 acre	equipment	Huron	14 acres	suspicious
	3 acres	debris burning	Iosco	.4 acres	power line
Alger	11 acres	powerline		.1 acre	children
Arenac	.1 acre	children	Iron	4 acres	debris burning
Baraga	5 acres	debris burning		5 acres	children
	.5 acre	incendiary		.1 acres	debris burning
Barry	1 acre	debris burning		.2 acres	debris burning
	.2 acres	incendiary		2 acres	equipment
	14 acres	incendiary		.2 acres	debris burning
	3 acres	debris burning		.2 acres	stove ashes
Chippewa	53 acres	debris burning	Jackson	25 acres	incendiary
	16 acres	debris burning	Kalkaska	.1 acre	debris burning
Clare	.1 acre	children		.1 acre	debris burning
	.3 acres	debris burning		5 acres	equipment
	.1 acre	debris burning		.1 acre	debris burning
	.2 acre	debris burning		.1 acre	campfire
Crawford	2 acres	debris burning	Kent	6 acres	debris burning
	4 acres	debris burning	Mackinac	3 acres	debris burning
	4 acres	children	Manistee	3 acres	debris burning
	30 acres	debris burning	Marquette	224 acres	equipment
Delta	5 acres	debris burning	Mecosta	30 acres	incendiary
	7 acres	debris burning	Menominee	6 acres	smoking
	.4 acres	children		.5 acre	railroad
	.2 acres	debris burning		2 acres	hot ashes
Dickinson	1 acre	debris burning		3 acres	debris burning
	1.5 acre	children		3 acres	debris burning

COUNTY	ACRES BURNED	CAUSE	COUNTY	ACRES BURNED	CAUSE
Menominee	.1 acre	debris burning	Ogemaw	.2 acres	debris burning
	.3 acre	incendiary		.1 acre	campfire
	1 acre	electric fence	Oscoda	.3 acre	debris burning
	3 acres	smoking		32 acres	debris burning
	.5 acre	debris burning	Ontonagon	.5 acre	debris burning
	5 acres	debris burning	Osceola	5 acres	debris burning
	2 acres	smoking		.1 acre	debris burning
	23 acres	debris burning		.1 acre	debris burning
Midland	1 acre	debris burning	Presque Isle	.2 acre	equipment
	4 acres	equipment		.2 acre	stove ashes
Missaukee	2 acres	smoking	Roscommon	3 acres	campfire
	30 acres	campfire		77 acres	campfire
Montmorency	44 acres	bonfire		.5 acres	children
Muskegon	4 acres	debris burning		120 acres	campfire
	1 acres	cutting torch	Schoolcraft	.5 acres	equipment
Oakland	4 acres	stove ashes	Tuscola	25 acres	debris burning
Oceana	.3 acres	debris burning		.5 acres	incendiary
	340 acres	campfire	Wexford	.1 acres	debris burning
Ogemaw	.2 acres	debris burning		.1 acre	debris burning
	2 acres	power line		.1 acre	debris burning
	.2 acres	power line		3 acres	children
	.2 acres	debris burning			

photo courtesy
Michigan DNR

Fire in the pines
▶

photo courtesy Michigan DNR

The aftermath of a forest fire—cabin and vehicle destroyed

Michigan Out-of-Doors
Wildfire Hotline Information
Smart Tips on Preventing Spread of Wildfires

To report a fire, call your Consolidated Dispatch Center at 911 or your local fire department. Limit calls to Consolidated Dispatch to only essential emergency communications.

All forest fires are investigated to determine origin and cause. Tickets are issued plus suppression costs charged. Anyone allowing a fire to escape is liable for damages caused by the fire. Incendiary (arson) fires are a serious cause of wildfires in Michigan. Anyone with information about a suspicious fire may call: Arson Hotline at 1-800-44-ARSON.

Art Sutton, Unit Leader, Resource Protection, Michigan DNR Forestry Division suggests the following wildfire prevention tips:

- Keep campfires small and never leave them unattended.

- Use an adequate amount of water, stir the ashes, then add more water when dousing a campfire. Turn all unburned wood over to wet down the underside.

- Keep brush or yard waste piles small and have a hose or water supply at hand.

- Never burn anything on a windy day.

- Supervise your children...many wildfires are started by unsupervised youngsters.

photo courtesy Michigan DNR

Smoke turns day into night

Robert Ziel, Resource Protection Unit, Forest Management Division, DNR, Marquette offers homeowners the following tips to help protect property from the threat of wildfire:

- Keep woodpile 25 feet from house and fuel tanks.
- Keep grass mowed 50 feet from any structure.
- Clear pines within 15 feet of any structure.
- Keep driveways accessible for fire trucks.
- Keep burnable materials from under/around all structures.
- Avoid outdoor burning.
- Keep 100 feet of garden hose attached to a water source.
- Keep the roof and rain gutters free of debris.
- Rake away leaves near outside of buildings.
- Cut excess small trees, brush and other dense fuels that burn rapidly.

Where We Are Now
January 20, 1999

by Arthur J. Sutton
Natural Resource Manager
Michigan Department of Natural Resources
Lansing, MI

Michigan has had a long history of wildfires and will likely continue to be plagued by the threat of uncontrolled wildfires. Every spring the snow melts and the dead grass and leaves from the previous year are exposed to the sun and drying winds. Sooner or later a lightning strike, a campfire left unattended, a spark from a burn barrel or burning leaf pile will start a wildfire. There isn't much we can do about the lightning strike but most of the others are fires that can be prevented.

The 1998 fire season lasted all year and was more severe than previous years. Department of Natural Resource personnel responded to 843 wildfires that burned more than 4,997 acres. That is about double the previous five-year average. Keeping track of fire information helps build a database that will help provide valuable information that can help prevent or reduce the losses caused by wildfire. What was the specific cause of the fire; was it caused by a permanent resident, seasonal resident, visitor; how was the fire detected; how big was the fire when detected; who detected it; what was the vegetation type; what kind of activity was involved in the fire start; and if possible, who started the fire? This is all information that is necessary to identify problem areas and develop programs that will reduce the number of wildfires and improve our ability to protect lives, property and our natural resources. To help in this effort, the new National Fire Incident Reporting System (NFIRS) has just gone online in Michigan and will soon be available across the nation. NFIRS will make it possible for both structural and wildfire agencies to have fire information recorded on one system. This should help give fire managers an opportunity to determine what the total wildfire problem is across the state and nation. Previously wildfire information from fire departments was sketchy at best. Fire Prevention is key to fire safety; a fire that is prevented does no damage.

We regularly monitor weather conditions as wildfire danger can be predicted by measuring temperature, humidity, wind speed and direction, and rainfall. During the winter of 1997–98, we reviewed information from the National Weather Service that indicated spring would be drier than normal. The Palmer Drought Index for 1997 showed the upper two thirds of the state ended the year with a substantial moisture deficit. The information also showed the effects that El Nino was already having on weather

Where We Are Now
by Arthur J. Sutton, Michigan DNR

DNR wildland firefighter mops up after a fire

systems in the Pacific Ocean. The prediction of warmer than normal temperatures and lower than normal precipitation amounts all pointed to the possibility of a severe spring wildfire season in Michigan. Firefighters across the state were well aware of the dry conditions but just how El Nino was going to affect the weather conditions was yet to be determined; everyone was bracing for a severe spring fire season.

The DNR Director K. Cool and his Management Team as well as the Governor's office were made aware of the possibility of a severe fire season. Contingency plans were developed to cover personnel, aircraft, equipment, supply and personal protective equipment needs. DNR Director Cool appointed his Press Secretary as liaison to the Forest Management Division to expedite any special media relations needs. A media plan was established that would permit a quick response to informational needs as the fire danger increased. Many news articles were sent to radio, television, and newspapers that helped make everyone aware of the increasing potential for forest fires. Information was provided on how to help prevent wildfires and how to help protect their own structures if a wildfire should occur. Making everyone aware of the fire danger is half the battle.

Finally, after many fires and several weeks of very high and extreme fire danger, on May 21, 1998, Governor John Engler, for the safety of all Michigan residents, ordered a Ban on all Open Burning. The Ban was in effect until June 3 and included all open burning of refuse, debris, brush, stumps, grass, stubble and crop residue, all campfires except those within containers or fire rings at authorized campgrounds, all smoking except in places of habitation, authorized campgrounds, or in automobiles or trucks. This was only the third time a governor has had to issue a statewide burn ban to ensure the safety of Michigan residents. It all helped. The number of debris burning and campfire caused wildfires decreased but lightning caused fires seemed to increase. Several thunderstorms with much lightning and very little rain contributed to this increase.

The year was developing into a serious fire season that required a total effort from the top down. Everyone made special efforts to ensure personnel and equipment were available to respond and assist with the necessary resources. Fire Suppression and support personnel were at a high state of alert during most of the spring and summer, as the El Nino influence was felt most of the year. By the end of December, DNR personnel had responded to 843 wildfires that burned 4,997 acres. Ninety-three percent of the wildfires were under ten acres with the largest being 1,252 acres. There were only seven fires over one hundred acres. Local fire departments assisted on many of these fires plus they suppressed many more grass and brush fires in their protection area without requesting assistance from DNR personnel. Personnel were quick to respond to every fire situation with prompt, aggressive, initial attack, because the longer it takes to begin the suppression action, the larger the fire gets and the more property and resources are endangered. Several fires required evacuation of the homes directly in the path of the fire. A few were damaged but none of the homes were lost.

Drought conditions persisted in some counties in the eastern Lower Peninsula, especially St. Clair County, where several different wildfires, during October and November, burned deep into the organic soils. Once the initial spread of the fire has been stopped, the job of completing the mop-up is very difficult. Each spot must be completely extinguished or it will dry the adjacent vegetation and continue to burn. These fires move very slowly but require the proper personnel and equipment to complete the job. To top it off, twelve fire departments were called to help battle a 134-acre wildfire in the Algonac State Park that burned during the evening of November 23, 1998. Burning after dark, the fire could be seen across the waters of Lake St. Clair and caused much concern by many residents of Detroit. The fire burned into mostly grassland and marsh but not before threatening several homes along the shore of the St. Clair River. Minor damage was sustained by three of the homes. Television crews in helicopters provided spectacular views of the fireline at night. Although not a large fire, it raised the awareness and interest of many people of the dry conditions Michigan experienced during 1998.

During the 30s and 40s Michigan made a conscious effort to move toward using equipment and machinery to assist in suppression of wildfires.

photo courtesy Michigan DNR

Algonac State Park Fire

Today the primary suppression unit is the Tractor-Plow, a bulldozer with brush protection and a rear mounted hydraulically operated v-plow. Our primary water units consist of 2½ ton 4x4 trucks equipped with brush protection, an 800-gallon tank and pump and a smaller rear mounted hydraulic v-plow. The workhorse is the converted military 6x6 equipped with a pump and a 1000 or 1500-gallon tank to aid in initial attack and mop-up operations. All units are radio equipped and the water units also have foam capability. These units are faster and much more efficient at building fire line than a firefighter with a shovel. Although there are times when the firefighter must rely on hand tools to complete a control line in difficult terrain or conditions.

Michigan is very fortunate to have the only state operated Forest Fire Experiment Station in the nation, located in Roscommon. The station was established in 1910 to develop, test and design various kinds of equipment to meet the needs of Michigan's complex fire problems. Testing of commercially available equipment is done to determine its effectiveness, safety, and durability in wildfire suppression. The station also designs, manufactures, and installs modifications to excess military vehicles for use as wildfire suppression vehicles. The Roscommon Equipment Center project is a subprogram in cooperation with the twenty northeast states, funded by a federal grant to research equipment projects of interest to these states. Recently the area of service has expanded to include the entire United States. A new facility is badly needed as we are still operating out of the same facility that was built in the 30s by members of the Civilian Conservation Corps. Many of the new commercial units will not fit into the main building to be modified for fire suppression duty. Commercial equipment manufacturers no longer supply the smaller bulldozers that are desired for fighting wildfires in Michigan. The bulldozers being manufactured now are larger, heavier, and much more powerful. But the problem is that these require larger storage and repair facilities, larger transport units, and redesign of the attached plowing equipment to match the power of the unit. The larger unit is also more difficult to maneuver between trees when used in fire suppression. We try to minimize the damage to the environment, thus the smaller units are often quicker and more efficient.

Where We Are Now
by Arthur J. Sutton, Michigan DNR

Without getting into specific amounts, the DNR Forest Management Division is trying to be good stewards of the funds made available for fire control in Michigan. Inflation has taken a major toll on the budget. An adequately funded equipment replacement budget would permit the replacement of fire suppression equipment on a twelve to fifteen year rotation schedule. Currently we have some equipment that is over twenty-five years old and need of replacement. Repair parts are often not available or difficult to obtain for these older units.

There is a major increase in technology now available to assist in various aspects of the wildfire program, however, that all has a price attached. The use of automatic weather stations provides up-to-date, timely weather information that is critical to providing the necessary data to fire managers responsible for staffing field stations and directing suppression efforts on wildfires. Automatic Vehicle Location (AVL) systems are expensive but are an essential way of keeping track of fire suppression vehicles that are working in heavy smoke on a wildfire. Satellite imagery and Geographic Information Systems can provide invaluable information about the area when fires occur. A much needed state-wide computerized wildfire reporting system will soon go on-line that will provide up-to-date information for fire managers.

This past year we contracted a Single Engine Air Tanker (SEAT) during May and June, to assist with wildfire suppression efforts in the Roscommon and Marquette areas. The SEAT is basically a crop dusting plan equipped with a 500-gallon tank, a foam injection system and a trap door that permits the pilot to drop the water/foam on the fire. It was expensive when compared to hourly rates for conventional equipment but was also very effective.

Often we are caught in the dilemma of determining whether to start initial attack or protect those structures in the immediate area. By protecting the homes and delaying initial fire suppression activity, the fire is allowed to get larger and possibly endanger many additional homes. The homes and cottages being built in the forest area compounds the problem for the firefighter. The results are an increased number of personal properties that require protection and increases in the possibility of wildfires starting in those areas as humans cause ninety percent of the wildfires. Burn barrels and the burning of yard waste, dead grass and leaves that have been raked into piles, are the number one cause of wildfires in Michigan. Use extra caution, get a burn permit from the local fire officials, don't burn on windy days and stay with the fire until it is out. The permit is generally free but it provides the fire official an opportunity to reinforce some safety precautions to the individual that is requesting the permit. The individual receiving the permit is still responsible for any damage caused by a fire that escapes their control and may also be charged for the cost of suppressing the fire.

All Forest Management Division personnel are trained in the basics of Incident Command System and all the fire suppression personnel have received advanced training in fire qualifications. Many have received additional training to qualify for dispatch under a national agreement for fire suppression duties throughout the United States as well as Ontario and Manitoba. There is a joint effort between the Department of Natural Resources, the Fire Fighters Training Council and local fire departments to provide necessary wildfire training and certification for local firefighters.

We are also developing the background data and information for a computerized Fire Simulator that will vastly improve our capabilities to train personnel in wildfire management. The system works on video disks and computer monitors and is capable of simulating actual fuel, weather, and fire conditions. It will be a valuable tool for all levels of fire training.

Limited budgets and reduced personnel numbers have resulted in a close working relationship with other fire agencies across the state; most are on a first name basis and know the capabilities of each of the partners. The DNR and U.S. Forest Service have consolidated their Air Detection flight plans to make fire detection more effective and efficient. The DNR is also a member of the Michigan Interagency Wildland Fire Protection Association (MIWFPA) and the Great Lakes Forest Fire Compact (GLFFC). MIWFPA was organized in 1981 to provide an effective and efficient wildfire prevention organization. The organization consists of the State Police Fire Marshal's Office, the Michigan State Firemen's Associa-

Where We Are Now
by Arthur J. Sutton, Michigan DNR

tion, the Michigan State Fire Chiefs, the USDA Forest Service; Ottawa, Hiawatha, and Huron/Manistee National Forests, the USDI Fish and Wildlife Service, Seney Wildlife Refuge, and the Bureau of Indian Affairs.

The Great Lakes Forest Fire Compact was organized in 1984 to promote effective prevention, presuppression, and control of forest fires in the Great Lakes Region. The exchange of technology, ideas, and resources has greatly improved the wildfire control efforts in the Great Lakes area. Members consist of the states of Michigan, Wisconsin, and Minnesota, and the provinces of Ontario and Manitoba.

We can muster a lot of manpower and equipment to suppress a forest fire but it is much easier and a lot less expensive when those fires are prevented. Please, before you leave be sure your campfire is dead out, don't burn on windy days, keep your engines properly tuned and clean up around your homes and building to prevent an oncoming fire from causing any unnecessary damage. Smokey Bear's message is still vital to fire protection. Only You Can Prevent Forest Fires. Please do your part to help.

Betty Sodders

Smokey the Bear sign—Raco Work Station, USDA Forest Service

Endnotes

Chapter 1

[1] J.A. Mitchell and D. Robson, *Forest Fires and Forest Fire Control in Michigan* (St. Paul: USDA Forest Service, 1950).

[2] *The Legacy of Roosevelt's Tree Army—The CCC in Michigan* and *Civilian Conservation Corps Museum Brochure* (Grayling: Michigan DNR).

[3] Charles A. Symon, *We Can Do It: A History of the CCC in Michigan— 1933-1942.*

[4] Gregory Lusk. Interview with author. Marquette, MI. 9 July 1993.

[5] Bill Main. Interview with author. East Lansing, MI. 17 April 1992.

[6] J.A. Mitchell and D. Robson, *Forest Fires and Forest Fire Control in Michigan* (St. Paul: USDA Forest Service, 1950).

Chapter 2

[7] J.A. Mitchell and D. Robson, *Forest Fires and Forest Fire Control in Michigan* (St. Paul: USDA Forest Service, 1950).

[8] Jim Pudelko. Interview with author. DeTour Village, MI. 11 November 1998.

[9] Unknown Michigan newspaper dated December 14, 1925.

Chapter 3

[10] Betty Sodders, **Michigan On Fire** (Holt, Michigan: Thunder Bay Press, 1997).

Endnotes

Chapter 4

Part One

[11] Lyman Beech. Interview with author. Tawas City, MI. 18 October, 1998.

Part Two

[12] Charles Van Wagner, "Age-class distribution and the forest fire cycle." *Canadian Journal of Forest Research* 8: 220-227.

[13] Lyman Beech. Interview with author. Tawas City, MI. 18 October, 1998.

[14] Donald A. Haines, "Horizontal Roll Vertices and Crown Fires," (East Lansing: USDA Forest Service, 1982).

Chapter 5

[15] *Wildland Firefighter* (October, 1997)

[16] Tom Kurtz. Interview with author. Raco, MI. 5 May 1994.

[17] Mobley, Jackson, Balmer, Ruziska, and Hough, *A Guide for Prescribed Fire in Southern Forests* (Atlanta: USDA Forest Service, 1973).

[18] Society of American Foresters, *Prescribed Burning: A Position of the Society of American Foresters* (1980).

[19] Schroeder, Glovinsky, Henricks, Hood, Hull, Jacobson, Kirkpatrick, Krueger, Mallory, Oertel, Reese, Sergius, and Wyverson, *Synoptic weather types associated with critical fire weather* (Office of Civil Defense, Office of the Secretary of the Army, USDA Forest Service, 1964).

Endnotes

[20] *Faces of Fire*, (Washington, D.C.: USDA Forest Service, 1996).

[21] "Controlled Fire Burns 450 Acres,"*Daily Mining Gazette*. 19 May 1978.

[22] Roswell K. Miller, "Report to the Fire Working Group of the Society of American Foresters" (Washington D.C.: 1977).

Chapter 6

Part One:

[23] Beverly Kleikamp, "The Seney Fire of '76 Becomes a Part of Michigan History," *Peninsula Press*, Vol. 1, Issue 6.

Part Two:

[24] Roswell K. Miller, "Yellowstone—Background and Synopsis of the Yellowstone Fires of 1988," (Houghton: Michigan Technological University).

[25] Luke Popovich, "U.P. In Flames...Taking Heat On the Seney," *Journal of Forestry (*March 1977): 147-150.

Part Three

[26] Roswell K. Miller, "The Keetch–Bryam Drought Index and Three Fires In Upper Michigan, 1976," Presented at the Fifth Joint Conference on Fire and Forest Meteorology and sponsored by the American Meteorological Society and the Society of American Foresters (Atlantic City: 14-16 March 1978).

Chapter 7

News clipping quoted from the following sources:
The Detroit News
The Crawford County Avalanche

Endnotes

Gaylord Herald Times
Houghton Lake Resorter
Roscommon Herald News
Oscoda County Herald
Traverse City Record-Eagle
North Woods Call, Petoskey

[27] Ronald Schwarz. Letter to author. Waters, MI. 23 January 1997.

[28] "Northern Michigan A Tinderbox—Firefighter Shortage," *Detroit News*, 25 June 1992.

[29] "Prospects For Forest Fires Are 'Very High'" *Bay City Times*, 7 May 1992.

[30] "Range Firing," *Crawford County Avalanche*, 7 May 1992.

[31] Gary Bouchelle. Letter to Lt. Col. Wayne Koppa. Roscommon, MI. 12 June 1992.

[32] *DNR News,* Lansing, 29 May 1992.

[34] Dan Alstott. Correspondence with Author. AuSable Manistee Action Council.

Chapter 8

[35] Don Johnson, "FIRE," *Michigan Natural Resources*, March/April 1991.

[36] Louis Borie, "Tragedy of the Mack Lake Fire," *American Forests*, July, 1981.

Endnotes

[37] Simard, Haines, Blank, and Frost, *The Mack Lake Fire* (St. Paul: USDA Forest Service, 1983).

[38] Richard P. Smith, "Regional Report," *Michigan Out-Of-Doors*, October, 1998.

[39] Tom Kurtz. Interview with author. Raco, MI. December 1998.

[40] Tom Opre, "Drought Conditions Worry Michigan's Forest Fire Staff," *Detroit Free Press*, 3 July 1988.

[41] National Wildland/Urban Interface Fire Protection Initiative, *Case Study: Mack Lake Fire* (Quincy, MA: National Fire Protection Association).

[42] "Chronology: Mack Lake Fire," (Lansing: USDA Forest Service).

[43] Donald A. Haines, "Horizontal Roll Vortices and Crown Fires" (East Lansing: USDA Forest Service, 1982).

Chapter 9

[44] David Jones, "Forest Blaze Injures Two in U.P." *Detroit Free Press*, 2 July 1988.

[45] Donald A. Haines, "Air Tanker Vortex Turbulence...Revisited," *Fire Management Notes* (1989 Volume 50, Number 2).

Chapter 10

Part One:
[46] J.A. Mitchell and D. Robson, *Forest Fires and Forest Fire Control in Michigan* (St. Paul: USDA Forest Service, 1950).

47 "Michigan's Forest Fire Experiment Station...What It Is: What It Does," (Lansing: Michigan DNR).

Part Two:
48 G.L. Stewart, "Of Fires and Machines" *Michigan Conservation,* 1955

49 Scott Harmsen, "This Think Tank Foists To Experiment With Fire," *Bay City Times*, 7 August 1988

50 Don Ingle and Brian Hutchins, "Michigan's Thin Edge Against Wildfire Disaster," *Michigan Natural Resources,* Sep/Oct 1993.

Chapter 11

Part One:
51 Northeast Forest Fire Supervisors, *Tanker Handbook, Military 5-Ton 6x6, 1,500 Gallon, Low Profile Tanker* (Roscommon: REC Program, 1987).

52 National Wildland/Urban Interface Fire Protection Initiative, *Case Study: Stephan Bridge Road Fire* (Quincy, MA: National Fire Protection Association, 1980).

Part Two:
53 National Wildland/Urban Interface Fire Protection Initiative, *Case Study: Stephan Bridge Road Fire* (Quincy, MA: National Fire Protection Association, 1980).

Part Three:
54 "Fire Losses Hit $3.5 Million," *Crawford County Avalanche*, 10, 17, 24, 31 May 1990.

Endnotes

[55] Jon Thompson and Irene Pettyjohn, "Fire Destroys At Least 50 Homes," *Crawford County Avalanche*, 10 May 1990.

Part Five:
[56] James Ricci, "Venerable Natives Surrender to Flame," *Detroit Free Press*,   25 June 1990

Chapter 12

[57] Humvee Specification Sheet (South Bend: AM General Corporation).

[58] Brian Hutchins. Interview with author. Roscommon, MI. 20 January 1994.

[59] Humvee Specification Sheet (South Bend: AM General Corporation).

[60] John Krzycki. Interview with author. Sault Ste. Marie, MI. 17 April 1998.

[61] Gregory Lusk. Interview with author. Marquette, MI. 28 March 1998.

[62] Northeast Forest Fire Supervisors, *Evaluating the HUMMER and HMMVW Series for Wildland Engine Use* (Roscommon: REC Program, Michigan DNR, 1987).

Bibliography

Books & Papers

Haines, Donald A., "Air Tanker Vortex Turbulence...Revisited," *Fire Management Notes.* Volume 50, Number 2, 1989.

Humvee Specification Sheet. South Bend: AM General Corporation.

Miller, Roswell K., "The Keetch–Bryam Drought Index and Three Fires In Upper Michigan, 1976," Presented at the Fifth Joint Conference on Fire and Forest Meteorology and sponsored by the American Meteorological Society and the Society of American Foresters. Atlantic City, 1978.

Miller, Roswell K., "Report to the Fire Working Group of the Society of American Foresters." Washington D.C., 1977.

Miller, Roswell K., "Yellowstone—Background and Synopsis of the Yellowstone Fires of 1988," Houghton: Michigan Technological University.

National Wildland/Urban Interface Fire Protection Initiative, *Case Study: Mack Lake Fire.* Quincy, MA: National Fire Protection Association.

National Wildland/Urban Interface Fire Protection Initiative, *Case Study: Stephan Bridge Road Fire.* Quincy, MA: National Fire Protection Association, 1980.

Northeast Forest Fire Supervisors, *Evaluating the HUMMER and HMMVW Series for Wildland Engine Use.* Roscommon: REC Program, Michigan DNR, 1987.

Northeast Forest Fire Supervisors, *Tanker Handbook, Military 5-Ton 6x6, 1,500 Gallon, Low Profile Tanker.* Roscommon: REC Program, 1987.

Bibliography

Society of American Foresters, *Prescribed Burning: A Position of the Society of American Foresters.* 1980.

Sodders, Betty, **Michigan On Fire.** Holt, Michigan: Thunder Bay Press, 1997.

Symon, Charles A., *We Can Do It: A History of the CCC in Michigan— 1933-1942.*

Periodicals

American Forests

Bay City Times

Daily Mining Gazette

DNR News

The Crawford County Avalanche

The Detroit Free Press

The Detroit News

Gaylord Herald Times

Houghton Lake Resorter

Journal of Forestry

Michigan Conservation

Michigan Natural Resources

Michigan Out-Of-Doors

North Woods Call

Oscoda County Herald

Peninsula Press

Roscommon Herald News

Traverse City Record-Eagle

Wildland Firefighter

Bibliography

Government & Research Reports

Haines, Donald A., "Horizontal Roll Vertices and Crown Fires." East Lansing: USDA Forest Service, 1982.

Mitchell, J.A. Mitchell and Robson, D., *Forest Fires and Forest Fire Control in Michigan.* St. Paul: USDA Forest Service, 1950.

Mobley, Jackson, Balmer, Ruziska, and Hough, *A Guide for Prescribed Fire in Southern Forests.* Atlanta: USDA Forest Service, 1973.

Schroeder, Glovinsky, Henricks, Hood, Hull, Jacobson, Kirkpatrick, Krueger, Mallory, Oertel, Reese, Sergius, and Wyverson, *Synoptic weather types associated with critical fire weather.* Office of Civil Defense, Office of the Secretary of the Army, USDA Forest Service, 1964.

Simard, Haines, Blank, and Frost, *The Mack Lake Fire.* St. Paul: USDA Forest Service, 1983.

"Chronology: Mack Lake Fire," Lansing: USDA Forest Service.

Faces of Fire, Washington, D.C.: USDA Forest Service, 1996.

The Legacy of Roosevelt's Tree Army—The CCC in Michigan and *Civilian Conservation Corps Museum Brochure.* Grayling: Michigan DNR.

"Michigan's Forest Fire Experiment Station...What It Is: What It Does." Lansing: Michigan DNR.

Index

Index

Index

Index

Index

Index

Index

Index

ABOUT THE AUTHOR

Betty Sodders was born and raised in Ironwood, Michigan, and lives on Sugar Island in the Upper Peninsula with her husband, Bill. A prolific and successful freelance outdoor and travel writer, her work has appeared in *Michigan-Out-of-Doors, Woods-n-Waters News, Whitetails Unlimited, Woodall's RV Traveler,* and many other publications. She is a member of the Outdoor Writers Association. *Michigan on Fire 2* is her sixth book.